Last of the Kriegies

Albert D. Gunn
51, SQadron
POW December 1943 - 1945
Stalag IVB

Last of the Kriegies

The extraordinary true-life experiences of five Bomber Command prisoners of war

Published in 2017 by Fighting High Ltd,
www.fightinghigh.com

British Library Cataloguing-in-Publication data.
A CIP record for this title is available from the British Library.

ISBN – 13: 978-0993415296

Designed and typeset in Adobe Minion 11/14pt
by Michael Lindley www.truthstudio.co.uk.

Printed and bound in Wales by Gomer Press.
Front cover design by www.truthstudio.co.uk.

Reflection *by Henry Wagner*

I do not think a man can ever be so lonely as when he is alone and hunted like an animal in a strange and hostile land, cold, wet and hungry, where he can be sure that every man's hand will be turned against him, some with murderous intent. There will be no help forthcoming from any quarter, he has no companion to support him, to talk things over with, to plan ahead. There is no thing or person besides him, he has nothing but his own resources, and he must stand alone on his own two feet. Although the chances of a happy outcome are remote, if in fact they exist at all, while there is life there is hope. It is raining and there is no shelter, but hang on in there.

Contents

Foreword

By Squadron Leader Bob Ankerson, RAF (Retd)

These five men are the representatives of the many thousands of their contemporaries who fought for our freedom in the Second World War. You will read recollections of hardship, deprivation, exhaustion and death. However, you will also find examples of many positive elements, including ingenuity, determination, humour, camaraderie and bravery.

I met some of these gentlemen with many of their fellow Kriegies some 26 years ago after I was a prisoner of war in Iraq in 1991 during Gulf War One. Soon after my release I received a letter from Air Commodore Charles Clarke inviting me to a formal dinner of the Royal Air Forces Ex-Prisoners of War Association. This event was the culmination of a five-day international reunion. As my wife and I, together with other Gulf POWs and their wives, were walking to the pre-dinner reception, we were asking each other why were we here to have dinner with all these veterans? Our ages ranged from early twenties to our forties, but the people we were about to meet were old enough to be our parents or even grandparents for some. On walking into the reception area we were greeted as old friends and that feeling has continued since. Although our shared experiences, as RAF aircrew and in captivity, were separated by time and our conditions of captivity were very different, that camaraderie from our RAF service and imprisonment meant there was an immediate mutual understanding between us. During that evening we exchanged experiences of fear, uncertainty, isolation, torture and loss of freedom. Many of the wives of the Kriegies mentioned that this was the first time they had heard much of what their husbands had experienced during the Second World War. You will read of tests of endurance and survival through their captivity, in particular in the winter of 1945 when the Germans marched the POWs for up to seven weeks in sub-zero temperatures, retreating from the advancing Russian troops. Many Kriegies only survived because of the determination of their friends to keep them moving.

I cannot imagine a more resourceful, optimistic group of people with a general sense of fun and a determination to enjoy the life that could so easily have ended during their captivity when they were in their late teens or early twenties. The recollections of these five RAF aircrew highlight characteristics of ingenuity and comradeship. While reading these compelling stories you are invited to remember the thousands of RAF prisoners of war who were repatriated, and those who died during their captivity.

Introduction

By Steve Darlow

On 24 March 2014 I had the pleasure of attending the seventieth anniversary commemoration of the 'Great Escape' at Stalag Luft III, Sagan, Poland. The weather was not good, but who were we to complain considering that seven decades previously, when the Allied escapees made their bid for freedom, the ground was blanketed in snow. The event was an international gathering of Allied veterans, government and air force representatives, relatives of Great Escapers, historians, serving airmen and enthusiasts to honour the anniversary of the extraordinary mass breakout of Allied prisoners of war.

Seven decades previously it had been an enforced international gathering of young men who had planned the audacious breakout. Stalag Luft III had been host to numerous airmen who had been shot from the sky as they fought in defiance of Nazism. They had become prisoners of the enemy they sought to defeat. But as Air Vice Marshal Stuart Atha, DSO, stated in his speech at the commemoration, they were 'not just prisoners of war but prisoners at war ... the men who escaped were not just any Tom, Dick or Harry'. Defiant to incarceration they had masterminded and engineered an escape plan and tunnel that had given them hope of freedom. Further speeches followed, paying tribute to the 'remarkable, ingenious men' and their 'character and courage'. Dignitaries recalled the 'extraordinary chapter in the history of our air forces', and asked us to remember 'these 76 young kids'. Air Commodore Charles Clarke, OBE, a former POW at Stalag Luft III addressed those present and symbolically cut the wire on a recently reconstructed goon tower. The act of commemoration closed with the last post, a minute's silence, reveille and a volley fire salute, at which point wreaths were laid at the memorialised exit to tunnel Harry. 'We will remember them.'

In the early hours of the following day, at the exit to tunnel 'Harry', fifty serving RAF personnel, representing each of their fated air force predecessors, awaited the order to begin their commemorative 110-mile march to the Poznan Old Garrison Cemetery, to pay their respects at the resting place of the murdered Great Escapers. POW veterans Charles Clarke and Andy Wiseman wished them well, and Andy reminded them that when they had evacuated the camp in January 1945 it was twenty-five degrees below, and they didn't have a lot to wear.

The commemoration was a truly memorable experience, and in the afternoon of 25 March I took the opportunity to visit the nearby 'Belaria' compound, where my grandfather Arthur Darlow had been held as a prisoner from May 1944 to January 1945. Using a map Arthur had drawn in his logbook and assisted by Monika Parker, a Polish lady who tirelessly works to maintain the memory of the POWs, David Dunn and a friend, we rummaged through the scrub and undergrowth, recovering bits of broken POW pottery, old bottles, an old toothbrush, a denture, and some ice skates – some of the detritus left behind when the compound was finally abandoned, and a physical link to the men incarcerated there all those years ago, and to my grandfather.

The visit to Sagan, the scene of the Great Escape, and Belaria compound was particularly moving at a personal level. The lot of the RAF prisoner of war has been an interest of mine for many years, and I have met and interviewed numerous former POWs, and also had the opportunity to publish their memoirs. In this book, I am delighted to present the stories of five more ex-Kriegies, who served with RAF Bomber Command and who I have had the pleasure to meet: pilot Reg Barker, bomb aimer Charles Clarke, air gunner David Fraser, air gunner Albert Gunn and navigator Henry Wagner. Each veteran shares the journey they went through after joining the Royal Air Force: their training and crewing up, and operational duties with RAF Bomber Command. We accompany them on raids over enemy territory as they fight to survive against the relentless flak, searchlights and deadly enemy night fighters. Eventually each airman's next of kin receives a knock on the door and the dreaded 'regret to inform you' telegram.

Reg, Charles, David, Albert and Henry describe the circumstances in which they are shot from the sky, descending by parachute into hostile territory, and their subsequent failed attempt to avoid capture. Interrogation follows and we hear how the downed airmen negotiate the aggressive and devious tactics employed by their captors as they try and extract secret information. Our 'Kriegsgefangener' soon find themselves behind the barbed wire of a German prison camp facing the trials and tribulations of daily life as a 'Kriegie': the battle with hunger and frustration, the baiting and harassing of prison guards, friendships made, and attempts to break out and escape their captivity. In the final months of the war some of our POWs endure the gruelling and harsh conditions of the forced 'Long March'. Despite frustrating delays, as the Nazi regime enters its final death throes, our airmen eventually taste the sweetness of liberation and journey home to loved ones and family.

David, Albert and Henry's story are sourced entirely from manuscripts they have written. Occasionally, to assist in the flow of the narrative, I have given some context to their accounts. Henry's story is based upon diary entries he wrote at the time, which he has either included in full or occasionally edited, combining these with his thoughts and reflections since the war.

Reg and Charles's stories are based upon face to face interviews, which I have transcribed, and also added, where necessary, respective context. I am also delighted that former Gulf War POW, Squadron Leader Bob Ankerson, RAF (Retd), agreed to write a foreword for the book. Bob continues to keep the memory of the POWs alive as secretary of the Royal Air Forces Ex-POW Association.

What follows is the extraordinary testimony of five RAF Bomber Command Kriegies who endured, and survived, being shot down, captivity, degradation and suffering. But *Last of the Kriegies* also reveals the extraordinary strength and resilience of the human spirit struggling with incarceration and a loss of freedom.

Steve Darlow *(July 2017)*

1	2	3	4	5	6	6	7	8	9	10	11	12	13	14	15

Name:

David Fraser

Bomber Command Air Gunner
Failed to Return from a 10/11 May 1941 Raid to Hamburg

Chapter One

Towards the Wire

The night of 10 May 1941 was clear, with a full moon, and as we approached our target, the Blohm & Voss works at Hamburg Docks, the flak increased in density. On our run up to the target, as we were about to release our bombs, there was a violent burst that destroyed any chance of accurate bombing. We decided therefore to make another attempt, which was more successful. As we turned away from the target and made for home, we were trapped in the beam of a blue-coloured searchlight and, immediately, several other lights locked on to us.

We then realised that we had been 'coned' and Andy, our skipper, took violent evasive action, but to no avail. We were well and truly caught, despite our desperate aerobatics, and the flak increased with great accuracy. I could hear and feel the shrapnel striking the aircraft and the reek of cordite indicated that the shell bursts were really on target.

Then suddenly the flak ceased and there was an ominous silence. We then realised that there was a night fighter in the vicinity; the searchlights were still holding us and Alex, our second pilot who was stationed in the astrodome (a Perspex blister on the top of the fuselage, used for observation purposes), called out, 'Look out for that fighter on the port quarter, Dave.' I could not see anything, as a flak burst had wrecked the hydraulic system to the turret, which was covered with hydraulic fluid, resulting in total opacity. When I attempted to swing the turret to engage the fighter, nothing happened, as my guns had been rendered useless by the lack of hydraulic pressure. My illuminated gunsight was non-existent. The fighter then fired a burst, which raked the port side of the aircraft and my turret. The escaped hydraulic fluid in the bottom of the turret ignited and the flames appeared near my right foot. I called to the skipper that my turret was on fire and he sent Bill, our navigator, to assist me with a fire extinguisher. By the time Bill arrived I had put the fire out by vigorous stamping, so I waved him back. Another burst from the fighter ignited the remaining flares in their rack and a raging inferno ensued. Andy then gave the order to bale out.

Normally I would have rotated the turret 90°, jettisoned the doors and dropped out backwards but, owing to the lack of oil pressure, the turret was immovable. Even the hand turning gear was useless. The turret had jammed so that only half a door's width was available for my exit towards the front of the aircraft. I managed to squeeze out of the narrow gap and into the fuselage where my parachute was kept, and made my way to the rear side escape hatch. Just as I reached it, another burst from the fighter struck the aircraft and it sounded like heavy hail on a tin roof. Alex was lying near the hatch and had managed to remove the cover. He was badly wounded, with blood oozing from his chest and arm. He was wearing his parachute, so I guided his hand to the D ring (which is pulled to release the chute) and stuffed him through the hatch. I then leaned out and, to my relief, saw his chute immediately open. I looked across to the main hatch and saw Bill bending over it. The hatch was open and he was obviously contemplating his exit. I then waved him farewell and dropped out into the night. I did not know at the time that, as Bill was returning to his position – after I had waved him away, having dealt with the fire in my turret – he was hit in the back by a burst from the fighter and, in his weakened state, he had dropped his parachute through the hatch.

But unaware of this I hastened to leave the aircraft and, after a very brief count of five, I pulled the ripcord. For a couple of seconds, which seemed like an eternity, nothing happened. Then the chute opened with a body-checking jolt and I was descending into the unknown.

I was falling smoothly, as there was no wind, when I heard the sound of an aircraft's engine, and a Messerschmitt 110 buzzed me and then immediately disappeared. I appeared to be falling towards a river and, in order to avoid a watery landing, I hauled on the shroud lines of my parachute to side-slip away from the river, which caused me to swing like a giant pendulum. The ground suddenly came rushing up at great speed and just before I hit the deck I swung forward and landed on the base of my spine.

As the speed of descent is akin to jumping out of a first-floor window without a chute, the resulting spine-shattering crash of my landing rendered me incapable of movement, so I just lay on the ground and gingerly moved all my limbs to ascertain whether there was any serious damage to my spine. While I was engaged in this exercise a herd of about fifty Holstein cattle approached and were sniffing around my discarded parachute. The type of terrain I had landed in was of a boggy nature and bore a great resemblance to Romney Marsh and, as there was no natural cover, I welcomed the concealment the cattle were providing.

So I just lay on the ground collecting my thoughts and listening to aircraft on their way home to safety and a welcoming at the de-briefing. I saw in the distance parts of a burning aircraft falling and, when I stood up, my back felt as though it had been run over by a heavy vehicle. I gathered up my parachute and stuffed it into a dyke until it sank, then contemplated making for the Danish border. But, as the Danes were occupied by the Germans, there seemed to be small hope of success in that direction; however, I pressed on in the direction of Denmark as there was a border that was worth looking at.

I was assailed by a feeling of utter loneliness, having been precipitated into an alien country where, undoubtedly, every man's hand would be against me. It was Fraser versus the Third Reich. This was followed by a sense of shock and horror. One moment we had been operating as an efficient crew in a perfectly serviceable aircraft and then, in a matter of minutes, the scene had been transformed into one of carnage and mayhem, with one of my comrades lying wounded in a blazing inferno, as I learned later.

Dawn was breaking when I stumbled into an area occupied by huts, obviously used by searchlight crews. I was about to steal away when a sentry spotted me, and raising his rifle to his shoulder, yelled 'Halt!.' I stopped dead in my tracks, and he walked over to me. I bade him 'Guten Morgen' and he said 'Ach, Engländer Flieger, for you the war is over.' He then motioned towards the hut, which I entered. There were several other German troops there and, lying on a table, was Alex. He looked in bad shape and was breathing rapidly and shallowly. There was blood oozing from a wound in his chest and his arm had also been hit. I asked the German NCO if there was a doctor nearby and he assured me that one had been summoned. I then spoke to Alex and he said, 'Look what they have done to my best shirt, Dave.' He raised his arm, which was bleeding under a bullet-ridden Van Heusen shirt sleeve.

I stayed for a few minutes until I was ushered into a waiting military truck, and there was Bernie, our front gunner, who had just been apprehended. I really thought that I would never see Alex again, as I feared he was dying. After a journey of an hour or so, we pulled up at the guardroom of a Luftwaffe station where we were given a breakfast of ersatz coffee, very dark rye bread and sausage, which I was unable to eat. Then we were driven to another part of the camp, where we were interrogated by a couple of officers who, to induce us to talk, made gestures that suggested hanging might be in the offing. I gave them my service number and my name and then clammed up. After a bout of shouting and further threats, a large car arrived, and we were driven to the Officers' Mess where we were regaled with coffee and cognac.

The officers were a pleasant lot, all with healthy suntans, obviously acquired in Spain, and brimming with self-confidence. They assured us that our stay in Germany would be for only a short time, as Germany would win the war within six months and England would be occupied. Their Führer, Adolf Hitler, would celebrate his victory with a grand parade, and he would head the parade on a white horse and occupy Buckingham Palace. We laughed and simply said 'Wait and see', which hugely amused the assembled company and there were many loud guffaws and scornful laughter.

When the time of our departure arrived, the whole Mess to a man turned out to see us off and, as we bade them farewell, they all chorused 'Wait and see'. I often wonder how many of them survived the war. I know one of them who achieved this because on the fiftieth anniversary of our downing, we met him in Germany. He was the pilot who had shot us down, and we learned that we were his first victims. He finished the war with a tally of thirty-six other victories.

We were driven to Hamburg railway station in a truck, accompanied by two guards who looked like a couple of music hall characters. One was over six feet tall, and skinny, and his greatcoat reached to just below his knees. He was armed with a small pistol in a minute holster. His companion was a short tubby individual whose greatcoat reached almost to his ankles, and his armament comprised a large revolver in an equally large holster. I felt affronted by these two, as I thought we merited guards of a much higher calibre.

We eventually boarded a train for Frankfurt am Main where we were met by two fresh guards in a truck and driven to Dulag Luft, which was the main reception and interrogation centre. I was placed on my own for about an hour, and then a Luftwaffe officer entered and proceeded to chat informally. He spoke perfect English without a trace of an accent, and his first words to me were 'Did you not compete against me at a university athletic meeting in 1939 in England?' When I answered in the negative, he produced a packet of twenty Players cigarettes which, as a non-smoker, I politely refused. He also handed me a bogus Red Cross form, inviting me to give the number of my squadron, so that he could then let them know that I was alive and well. I returned the form and stated my name, rank and service number and resolutely refused to provide him with any further information. So I was confined to a room and left for some hours.

Chapter Two

Before the Wire

During four or more hours of absolute confinement, I had ample time to reflect on previous events and my life in the Royal Air Force.

I had joined the RAF at the age of seventeen and a half on 6 February 1939. The war was becoming increasingly imminent and, although I had been a gunner in the Royal Artillery Territorial Army, I was driven by my boyhood dreams of flying.

I enlisted as a flight mechanic, on the assumption that I would be able to learn a trade and fly as part of the job, and travelled up to London for the necessary medical and educational tests. I had no trouble with the medical test as I had always kept really fit and was neither a smoker nor a drinker. The education test was a simple affair, comprising a few grammatical questions and an essay. In the latter I really extended myself and wrote quite a lengthy work, which really impressed the flight sergeant in charge of the candidates and he asked me if I really wished to enlist as a flight mechanic. I was fully aware that maths was my weak subject and I resolved to remedy this deficiency once I was in the service.

Within a week or so I received a travel warrant and instructions to report to RAF West Drayton, which was the reception depot in Middlesex where, at all times, there seemed to be a motley collection of people milling around. I soon realised that this was the mass productive flow of recruits, brought about by the impending war.

On the second day we were attested and then we became sworn members of His Majesty's Forces and were, to a man, volunteers. We were issued with a knife, fork and spoon and at meal times we lined up in an orderly queue, which kept moving, and received our food from the servers standing behind the various dishes on offer. After the meal, we left the dining hall and washed our plates and eating utensils in one of two huge containers of hot water. The plates were then left to be collected, but we retained our knives, forks and spoons for future use.

On day three we were assembled in various batches for dispatch to our allotted training establishments. Our party was destined for Brize Norton in Oxfordshire and we arrived there during the afternoon. This was the base where we would spend the next eight weeks, undergoing a rigorous drilling (square bashing) and physical training regime, designed to convert us into real airmen.

Upon arrival we were allocated to one of several barrack huts in parties of twenty-four. We were all standing around the cylindrical stove in the centre of the hut when the door burst open and a burly corporal entered, with the words: 'They call me S— the bastard, and bastard I'll be if you don't shape-up and look lively.' He was a physical training instructor and there was one of these at the end of every hut, where they had an individual bunk. This man was not our instructor, however, but happened to be passing as we arrived and thought he would instil the fear of God into us. And, thus, the tone was set for the duration of our stay.

Before we started on the training programme, we had to attend a kitting-out parade, where we were issued with our new RAF uniforms. This procedure was a hilarious occasion, as men of all shapes and sizes tried on the various items of kit. In most cases everyone managed to find something that would fit. The visit of the camp tailor the next day completed the outfitting to most people's satisfaction. There were, though, one or two awkwardly shaped chaps who failed to find anything at all to suit, and they had to await the arrival of specially tailored uniforms. I particularly remember one man who was tall, awkward and peculiarly shaped. He had arrived wearing a suit of green plus-fours, and the only items of uniform which fitted him were a hat, a webbing belt, and a large pair of issued boots, which he wore for the next three weeks until his personally tailored clobber arrived.

For the first four weeks of the course, we were confined to the camp and were not allowed to set foot outside the gate until we could 'conduct ourselves like real airmen'.

My military experience and training in the Territorial Army as a gunner in the Royal Artillery enabled me, as a keep-fit enthusiast, to take the routine physical training and drill in my stride. We were a squad of thirty-two men and the NCO in charge of the whole programme was a very vociferous flight sergeant. We had one extremely inept member of the squad, who was so uncoordinated that he was unable to march in unison with the others. On one occasion the flight sergeant became incensed at his shortcomings and called the squad to a halt. 'What's your name?' he thundered, and the misfit replied 'L—', whereupon the flight sergeant roared 'L— what?' When the poor chap answered with 'L— Tim', instead of 'L— Flight Sergeant', the latter yelled 'For God's sake let's have a whip round and buy the silly bugger out.'

The bed next to mine was occupied by one Rocky G who was a mature chap of twenty-four. We became firm friends, especially as he boxed and played rugger for Burton RFC in the Midlands. The other two members of our group were Canadians, and we four spent most of our spare time together in the camp gym, boxing, training and generally keeping fit. I was not yet eighteen and Rocky became my mentor.

At the end of our four weeks' isolation period, we were allowed into the outside world.

Sunday church parades were a very informal affair and we used to march to the small village church where the vicar took the service and his wife played the organ. We were amused and amazed when, at the end of the service, the good lady played us out to the strains of 'Under the Spreading Chestnut Tree'. We then repaired to the adjacent pub, where we joined the vicar and his dear lady in a welcome glass of good ale. Our group of four would then walk back past the camp to the next village of Carterton, where we had a ploughman's lunch at the Beehive, instead of the Sunday camp fare. This became our ritual on most Sundays, and very pleasant these days were. I never drank more than a half-pint of ale, so my introduction to beer was gradual. The pints followed in due course.

Our PTI, a corporal, was a wiry, bow-legged individual with a particularly rasping voice who took great delight in exercising his authority whenever possible. Most of the recruits stood in awe of him and cringed when they were in earshot of that sandpaper voice. One of the members of our squad was, in Civvy Street, a cub reporter and a man of the world. One day, he collected the mail for the hut and there was a letter for our corporal, whose address bore his Christian name. We had just finished a session of PT and were taking a breather when F—, with a flourish and in a very loud voice, declaimed 'Here's your mail Robert', at which effrontery F— was ordered to complete five laps of the sports ground. By the time he had finished his punishment he was in a state of collapse and staggered to the showers to recover. My dear wife, who joined the WAAFs in 1941, did her square bashing at Blackpool and the man in charge of the recruits' drilling was none other than our old corporal, but now elevated to the rank of warrant officer.

On the last day of the course we had a passing out parade and in the evening there was a special passing out dance. The females for this occasion were bussed in from the surrounding district and Rocky's girlfriend was in full evening dress. They cut a great dash – and Rocky did not return to camp until the next day. We were then granted seven days' leave, after which our group of four, together with eight other chaps, were posted to RAF Stradishall in Suffolk, pending the start of our technical training course at Hednesford, Staffs.

Stradishall was a bomber station, equipped with Wellington aircraft. There was no runway and the aeroplanes could barely clear the airfield on take-off, with only half a crew and no bomb load. This situation was soon remedied, however, by the removal of the squadron to the racecourse at Newmarket while the hard runway was constructed. We were employed in filling sandbags with earth and building airfield defence works in the form of gun pits etc. I had been at Stradishall for only two weeks when I contracted German measles and was transported by ambulance to the isolation hospital at RAF Halton, Bucks, where I remained for three weeks. Upon my return to Stradishall, Rocky and the two Canadians organised a night out as a celebration and we enjoyed a riotous evening. A marvellous time was had by all, which culminated in our putting Rocky to bed on his own in a barrack hut, together with a goat that we had discovered grazing nearby. The next morning Rocky described how he had woken up during the night on the floor between two beds, with the goat licking his face, and he thought he was having a nightmare.

In due course, we were posted to RAF Hednesford, Staffs, for technical training and Rocky and the two Canadians were posted elsewhere. Here we learned the mysteries and intricacies of the internal combustion engine, and were instructed on radial and in-line aircraft engines. The surrounding country was rugged and provided good cross-country running territory, so I often took off for a three-mile or six-mile run. I teamed up with a north-country chap and we used to walk to some nearby lakes for a swim. On Sundays we would walk a couple of miles to a roadside café, which catered for cyclists, and, for the sum of one shilling and sixpence, we enjoyed a splendid tea of bread, butter and jam and a variety of cakes.

We were at Hednesford when, on Sunday morning 3 September, war was declared on Germany. The whole camp was agog with excitement and it was rumoured that we were moving on to pastures new. The following week was all hustle and bustle and we were inoculated with a wide range of anti-disease drugs, on the assumption that we may have to serve anywhere in the Empire. After the injections we asked a veteran sergeant for the best course to follow, and he advised us to take plenty of exercise. We promptly grabbed our swimming gear and headed for our favourite lakes, where we swam for about an hour. This seemed to work for us, because when we returned to camp, there were people lying around on their beds, prostrate and groaning, with swollen arms and looking really ill.

Later in the week we were informed that we were moving to St Athan in South Wales, where there was a technical training school for our benefit. There we were issued with two pieces of steel and a file. The metal comprised two blocks of steel, one of which had a square aperture in its centre, the female part, while the other component was in the form of a block. Our task was to file each component part so as to achieve a flush fit when the block was inserted into the square orifice of the female part. I rapidly became bored to death with the whole concept of this type of engineering and my whole being craved the chance to fly. I was so desperate that I absolutely refused to treat the grade test seriously, with the result that my pieces of metal, instead of fitting snugly together, wobbled about in a most unsatisfactory manner.

I thought that my effort (or lack of it) would mean that I would fail the course. However, when I went before the commanding officer at the final interview, he refused to fail me and I passed, albeit with drooping colours, at the lowest possible mark of 40%. He understood my plight and advised me to re-muster to aircrew duties at my next unit. I was posted to RAF Cranwell in Lincolnshire. The accommodation was in established barrack blocks, which were constructed in the early thirties and we were twelve to a room on the ground floor.

The winter of 1939/40 was a vicious one. It snowed and froze for weeks. There was no flying for seven weeks and we were employed in keeping the camp roads and footpaths clear. With the advent of spring, life returned to normality, and the flying training programme went ahead with a flourish. The pupil pilots were destined to fly bombers, and the aircraft in use at the Flying Training School were twin-engined Airspeed Oxfords. It was our job to maintain them and keep them sufficiently fed with fuel at all times.

The Command boxing championships were to be held in March, so I started training in preparation for the event. I was still only eighteen years old and had three nights of boxing: two fights on each of the first two nights with the final on the third night. On the first night I won, but on points, and the other one was stopped in my favour. On the second night I won both of my bouts by KOs. The final fight was stopped, again in my favour – and so I became the Command light-heavyweight champion. Our boxing coach, a former RAF heavyweight champion, applauded my efforts and assured me that, under his guidance, I could achieve a very high standard of skill. As it happened, I was unable to take advantage of his offer, as later in the year I volunteered for aircrew training and was posted to a gunnery school in Scotland. I never did box again, apart from one or two sparring sessions with aspiring pugilists in German prison camps.

Night flying was part of the curriculum and, for this purpose, we used an airfield some miles from Cranwell. It was literally a large field without a hard runway. The flare-path – the strip of land used for take-off and landing – was illuminated by paraffin-fuelled torches housed in metal containers that were placed at fifty-yard intervals in two parallel lines, as a guide for aircraft taking off and landing. These flares had to be kept alight permanently during flying times and it was our duty to maintain them. We had to patrol the flare-path and be ready to remedy anything that might cause them to fail. This entailed keeping them charged with fuel and replacing those displaced by violent contact with landing aircraft. This was a risky job and one had to be ever watchful in order to avoid being struck by incoming aircraft. Although we were suitably clad to withstand the winter night air, it was still a chilling job.

At some time during July 1940 a notice appeared on the station Routine Orders Board, inviting applications for the posts of pilot, navigator and air gunner. On enquiring for details, I was informed that the training for pilots and navigators involved months, while that for air gunners was only a matter of weeks. As I did not want to miss the war, I applied for an interview with a view to train as an air gunner and within two weeks I attended a selection board. It was conducted by three officers, one of whom was a medical officer, and was completely oral. The questions were of a general knowledge and mathematical nature and I had no difficulty with any of them. I then had to blow into a tube connected to a scale containing mercury, and maintain the blowing pressure for as long as I could. My effort seemed to satisfy the medical officer who then proceeded with his physical examination. I was then dismissed and told that I would be advised in due course.

During the summer we had the Cranwell Command Sports Day and I was entered for the three-mile race and the javelin throwing. It was a typically wonderful summer's day and the sports ground was crowded. I had just made my first throw when I noticed the runners gathering for the start of the three-mile race and, by the time I had completed my throwing, the starting pistol had been fired and the runners were off. I dashed over to the now vacant starting point and was encouraged to join the runners, who were already some thirty yards ahead, so I gritted my teeth and grimly set about what seemed to be an impossible task. However, I finally caught up with the field and was content to keep my place at the end of the tail, until I had established a steady breathing rhythm. The race comprised twelve laps and, at the end of the first lap, I had overtaken five or six of the back markers. As the race progressed I was pleased to see some competitors dropping out. At the end of each lap the field thinned until, at the start of the final lap, I was lying second to the leader, a member of my flight who played football for the RAF. Despite my last minute efforts I was unable to catch him and I finished second, about twenty-five yards behind him. The event was a good one for my flight and we ended the day with the highest number of points. This called for a celebration and that evening we repaired to the NAAFI for the evening festivities. I am afraid that, for the first time in my life, I was sloshed, having consumed a number of celebratory pints. I was absolutely legless. The air-raid siren sounded and everyone made for the shelter nearby. I was absolutely incapable, so Cyril Washbrook, the England Test Match cricketer who was a physical training instructor, picked me up, slung me over his shoulder, and bore me to the shelter where I gradually sobered up. Years later, after the war, I met him again when he was playing for Lancashire against Kent at Tunbridge Wells and we had a good natter about the Cranwell days.

One Saturday in September a friend and I travelled by car to Nottingham, intending to return by bus. However, due to a misunderstanding we missed the bus and were then faced with a twenty-six-mile walk back to camp. Fortunately, it was a fine night and we had covered about three miles when we saw a vehicle approaching, travelling in our direction. Naturally, it had no proper headlights because of wartime restrictions on the showing of lights. It therefore relied on masked headlights, which were merely slits cut in the masking. We signalled frantically, as in those days there was not much traffic about due to the petrol shortage and this could well have been our only chance of securing a lift. The car stopped and, to our amazement, it was festooned with people hanging on the outside of the vehicle. There were three people in the front seat, including the driver, with three in the back seat and two on the floor, as well as a body clinging on to each front mudguard. My friend clambered on to a carrier at the back and I managed to hoist myself on to the roof and hung on for dear life. It was a Ford Ten and was carrying twelve people. The car then restarted its journey to Newark, some eight miles ahead, and we arrived safely after a slow jaunt, because of the unusual load. This still left us with a journey of twelve miles to Cranwell. It was now early on Sunday morning so we doggedly tramped on and were finally welcomed back at base in time for Sunday breakfast.

That Sunday, 15 September, is indelibly stamped on my memory, as it marked a significant phase in the Battle of Britain, when Goering marshalled his Luftwaffe to destroy the RAF. The German losses inflicted by our fighters forced the enemy to re-think their air war strategy and they then began a night bombing programme.

In October I was informed that my application to re-muster to aircrew had been successful and that I would be posted to a gunnery school in due course. My heart leaped for joy and, due to the elation and anticipation, I found it difficult to eat or sleep and relaxation was impossible. I was detailed to draw my flying kit from the store and required another kit bag to contain the extra clothing. Thus it was, that in the last week of October 1940, I was posted to No. 8 Bombing and Gunnery School at Evanton in Scotland on the Cromarty Firth. With the approach of winter the weather showed signs of becoming decidedly chilly. We appeared to be miles from civilisation and our main source of entertainment was the NAAFI. We were allocated to one of several wooden structured huts and thus our spartan way of life began.

The day started at 06.30 hours with the door of the hut flying open and the entrance of a stentorian-voiced physical training instructor, bouncing a football on the bare boards of the floor and yelling as he pranced up and down the hut, threatening any laggards with all manner of punishment. Having risen, we donned our gym vests, shorts and plimsolls and gathered together in the hostile frost-laden air. We were then subjected to a series of exercises, which culminated in running several circuits of the camp, after which we were dismissed and exhorted to take a shower, which was invariably cold. This regime did not bother me, but some of my fellow trainees found the going tough and staggered rather than ran round the circuit. This programme was enforced during the whole of the four-week course, at the end of which everyone emerged fitter and happier.

Our days were fully occupied with lectures and gun-handling sessions, as well as time in the armoury where we stripped and cleaned guns and filled ammo pans with .303 rounds, which we fired off during our flying sessions. The flying was in clapped-out Handley Page Harrows of 1937 vintage and Fairey Battles, the latter being a so-called fighter-bomber that became obsolete after the fall of France, where dreadful losses in first-class aircrew and aircraft were suffered. The lumbering Harrow was so slow that, against a stiff breeze, it almost hovered. I remember on one occasion when we were returning from an exercise, we flew along and over the high street of the local town at about 500 feet. I was in the rear turret and I distinctly saw the local policeman on point duty take his notebook out of his pocket, look up, and write something down. He was taking our number and when we returned to base our pilot was given a good rollicking by the CO.

The pilot was Polish and was browned off to the hilt with his lot in life. There were several Polish pilots at the base, engaged in the monotonous task of ferrying trainee gunners and navigators about the sky. They were usually fighter pilots who had been found guilty of indiscipline while flying with fighter squadrons. Their usual crimes were breaking formation to pursue a German aircraft. Having to fly us around was their punishment, before returning to their respective squadrons. They hated the Germans with a fanatical loathing and, in view of the Polish people's ill-treatment and the ethnic cleansing, they had good reason for their attitude. We had a Polish pilot on one exercise, which was air-to-air firing, and while we were waiting for the drogue-towing aircraft to appear, he flung the Fairey Battle all over the sky. It was his means of keeping his hand in, pending return to his squadron.

On another occasion I was in a Harrow, waiting my turn to fire, when there was a loud cracking sound and I looked around to see what was happening, only to be confronted by a view of the countryside. A considerable area of the fuselage was bereft of fabric, as a long strip had blown off the airframe and was flowing in the slipstream like a huge pennant.

Owing to the strenuous work programme, we had no time for 'pubbing' during the week, so any drinking time was spent in the NAAFI. The weekends, however, were different and on Saturday nights we repaired to the local hostelry for our recreation. The result was a solid jam-packed crowd and we were lucky if the pints we ordered ever reached us. One evening I was in the crowd, waiting for the arrival of the beer, when another group of bods, heading for the exit, squeezed past me. Among them was an old school mate whom I had not seen for five years. We had no chance to chat as, by sheer weight of numbers, they were propelled towards the door. Some years after the war, I was visiting my old home town of Chepstow and had a few silent moments at the local war memorial. There, included among the names of boys I had been to school with, was the name of the fellow I had not had the chance to talk with, all those years ago, in a packed Scottish pub.

On 30 November our course finished and we were awarded our sergeant's stripes and air-gunner's brevets, as qualified air gunners. With great pride we hurriedly sewed these adornments on to our best blue tunics. We were then paid and granted fourteen days' leave.

The next phase of our training programme was a posting to No. 20 OTU (Operational Training Unit) at Lossiemouth, Scotland. On the day of our arrival we were greeted by the spectacle of a Vickers Wellington crash-landing and bursting into flames. Fortunately, there were no casualties, but the incident was forever stamped on our minds. The living accommodation was wooden huts divided into rooms (bunks), which we shared with one other person. My bunkmate was Jimmy James, a Welshman from Cardiff, and from our first meeting we hit it off. He was a diminutive individual, around 5 feet 3 inches in height, with a great sense of humour. Before re-mustering to air gunner, he had been a corporal in charge of a telephone exchange. In order not to alarm his parents when he went home on leave, he used to remove his brevet and tell them that he was a ground gunner on the station defence strength. Unfortunately, Jimmy was shot down over the sea on a Brest daylight raid and, when his parents were advised of his death, they travelled up to where he was stationed to see his body, only to learn the terrible truth of the matter. Owing to the influx of training personnel, the permanent Sergeants' Mess was unable to accommodate us, so we had our own trainee Mess in the form of a large hut. In our bunk the heating was provided by a small, solid-fuel stove and the supply of coal was totally inadequate for a winter in Scotland. We therefore had recourse to the odd raid on the main coal yard, which necessitated climbing a six-foot-high brick wall. We were aware of the Sergeants' Mess's cheerful blaze in their fireplace, so we bore no guilt feelings about purloining the odd bucket of coal from the main supply.

We spent Christmas Day in the time-honoured fashion whereby, before we sat down to our dinner, it was our duty to wait upon and serve in the Airmen's Mess. All went well until I approached one airman who held out his plate and appeared to be complaining about something. I peered closely at his plate but could see nothing untoward with the contents. Then, to my relief, he loudly declaimed that there was not enough on it. I therefore heaped it up and pressed on with my duties.

At the time, there was panic in the air in the form of an invasion alert and some idiot had conceived the idea of a defence scheme that involved all aircraft to be parked against the sea wall in a defensive ring, so that all gunners would occupy their turrets and deliver a beam attack on any invading troops appearing over the wall. This meant running the engines of the aircraft to supply the hydraulic pressure to turrets and guns, with the consequent overheating of the engines and the subsequent failure of hydraulic pressure. It would have been a far better idea to have taken off, bombed up somewhere, and returned to bomb and strafe the enemy. In the event, nothing happened and the course continued without further interruption.

The weeks were occupied with lectures, aircraft recognition sessions and gun-handling and maintenance classes until the end of 1940 drew near. It was during the afternoon of New Year's Eve that Wellington No. N2980, while on a navigation exercise, ran into trouble in a snowstorm, followed by engine failure. They happened to be over water – Loch Ness, as it happened – so the skipper ordered the pupils to bale out. He and the co-pilot then successfully brought the aircraft to rest on the water and made a textbook exit before the aircraft sank into the depths of the loch.[1]

On the evening of that fateful day (New Year's Eve), Jimmy and I decided to walk to Forres, some five miles away, for a celebratory evening at the main hotel where we arrived at about 8pm after a pleasant walk. We thoroughly enjoyed the Scottish festivities until nearly 1am, when we decided to return to base, but on opening the front door of the hotel we were confronted by a covering of snow nearly two feet deep. However, buoyed by the amount of scotch we had consumed during the evening, we pressed merrily on, in good spirits, so to speak. There was a breeze blowing that was causing the snow to drift in places and, as we progressed, the snow grew deeper and was forming large drifts, some of which were three or four feet deep. I walked ahead and acted as a human snowplough so that the diminutive Jimmy could make some progress in my wake. But some of the drifts were waist deep and it became impossible for him to make any progress at all. I then had to piggyback him as far as these drifts extended. On one occasion I carried him for half a mile before we came to shallower snow. Some three hours later we arrived back at base, somewhat knackered and very damp in the nether regions, but we quickly got a fire going in the bunk and piled on as much coal as we could. We then removed our sodden uniforms, had a brisk towelling, donned pyjamas, made a hot drink and retired for what was left of the night.

One day in March we were told to assemble in one of the hangars, and when we arrived there the building was crowded with trainee aircrew. We were encouraged to mingle and associate freely with each other. This was the accepted practice then of crew selection by free consent. Within a few minutes, two wireless operators approached me with a view to my joining them and, as they seemed to be reasonable types, I complied. Then we were joined by a very jovial and likeable navigator (observer in those days). He said that he had found two pilots. These two individuals were Australians, Pilot Officer Alan McSweyn and Sergeant Alex Kerr. We all seemed to hit it off, so we decided to become a crew. The wireless operators were Geoff Hogg and Bernie Morgan and the observer was Bill Legg from Weymouth in Dorset. We eagerly awaited the start of the flying programme.

It was at this time that the air gunners and wireless operators/air-gunners on the course were moved into Lossiemouth, where we occupied a rather pleasant house overlooking the sea and the golf course. We attended the local Saturday night dances in the town and it was at one of these that I met the daughter of the resident golf professional, a one-time Scottish champion. I had never played golf, but Veronica induced me to try it – and what a pleasant pastime it proved to be. We had the run of the golf club shop at the course and she said that her father would give me some lessons in due course. The second tee was overlooked by the house in which we were billeted and, whenever I attempted to drive off, there was always a group of fellow gunners at an open window urging me to hit the bloody ball and jeering like mad when I messed up the shot. How very off-putting it all was.

Veronica had a friend with whom I enjoyed many long walks. One day, on one of our jaunts, we passed close to a property owned by the Duke of Hamilton; I think it was his shooting lodge, although it was quite an impressive building where she had been to one or two parties. She mentioned that Rudolph Hess, Hitler's deputy, had visited the duke before the war. On 10 May 1941, while we were winging our way through the night to bomb Hamburg Docks, Hess was making his way to Scotland in a Me110 fighter-bomber to contact the duke with a view to striking a deal with our government and arranging a peace deal. Herr Hess bailed out in open country, near the duke's residence, and was soon arrested, interrogated and imprisoned. The rest is history.

Our operational flying training commenced on 17 March 1941. There were six crews per course and we invariably lost one crew before completion of the course. These losses were due mainly to the clapped-out state of the aircraft and extreme weather conditions. The ground staff worked like trojans, at all hours of the day and night, to keep us airborne, but the silk purse and sow's ear syndrome unfortunately prevailed. During one trip over the Western Isles, we were caught in an electrical storm and, flying through a snowstorm, our instruments failed. We had no means of knowing our height or direction so Alan decided to maintain the direction in which we were flying before the instruments went haywire. I was keeping a wary lookout from my turret when, to my consternation, I was aware of snow-clad terrain rushing past. I immediately yelled 'Climb, climb' and we passed over the top of the Isle of Eigg with only about 300 feet to spare. Fortunately, the instruments returned to normal and we arrived safely back at base.

On another occasion, we were preparing to land and, as we touched down, I was aware of an unusual sideways lurch of the aircraft. The tail was on the ground and describing a very wide arc at a great speed. As I was at the extremity of the aircraft, I felt the full effect of the centrifugal force. We had hardly stopped before an ambulance and fire engine were at the scene and, upon our arrival at the crew room, we were greeted by the station medical officer who asked us whether we would fly again. As the answer was in the affirmative, he heaved a sigh of relief and disappeared. It was Alex who was at the controls and he correctly selected undercarriage to 'down' with the appropriate lever, but due to malfunction, only one leg extended, hence our landing on one wheel.

Another time, while we were away on a night trip, the wind had veered so that what was a favourable wind for take-off, had become a tailwind on our return and the ground staff had failed to make the necessary adjustment to the flare-path. As a result we finished up about fifteen yards from the sea wall.

During the last flight of the course, at night, we were on the second leg of our route towards Aberdeen, when we saw flares over the sea. We were most concerned as one of our crew had taken off just before us on the same course. The weather was broken cloud with a half moon. We flew in the direction of the flares and began to lose height, all the while circling the area. After searching for a quarter of an hour I caught sight of a dark blob on the water, which looked as though it could have been a dinghy. Bill, our observer, had worked out the position of the dinghy; Geoff got a message back to base and, on our return, we were congratulated on a commendable crew effort. This dinghy was proved to contain the downed German crew of a Junkers 88, which had been intruding at Montrose. It was a fitting example of the skills we had honed during the course and the wing commander, who was returning to operations, tried to commandeer us as a crew. We dug our heels in and he had to select another crew.

The food at the base was appalling – in particular the flying suppers. The crunch came when, one evening, the fare comprised a sausage roll (cold) covered by warm gravy in an attempt to redress the balance. This was too much and the next day we convened a meeting of all trainee aircrew to decide a course of action. We decided to form our own Mess and, with this in view, our delegates approached the station catering officer who, after a brief discussion, consented to our suggestion. The result was, in return for a regular payment from us, he would undertake to provide a reasonable flow of decent ingredients. The food improved immediately and we were a far happier bunch of fliers, although we were only able to enjoy two weeks of this improvement before the course ended.

Of the six rear gunners who completed our course within two years four had been killed in action and the remaining two, including myself, had become POWs.

We were granted seven days' leave, at the end of which we were posted to RAF Station Marham in Norfolk, which is about twelve miles from King's Lynn. We were disappointed to learn that Alan, our skipper, was to be assigned to an experienced crew for six trips, after which he would return to us. It made sense, but we never did enjoy the experience of the man who was a fine skipper, and in whom we had complete confidence, for he was shot down on 29 June 1941. We were allocated to A Flight at Marham and the squadron commander was Wing Commander

Evans, a huge, jovial, avuncular figure who was immensely popular with his crews. When we were introduced to him he was hobbling about with one leg encased in plaster, the result of having to bale out when returning to base from an operation in thick fog that had covered a great part of the country that night and during which several crews had had to abandon their aircraft over home territory.

We were also introduced to our new skipper, John 'Andy' Anderson, a Scot from Aberdeen who was entirely different in character from Alan, in that he was rather introverted and withdrawn, whereas Alan was an extrovert and completely in touch with all aircrew members at all times. Our first flight with the squadron was a two-hour cross-country exercise, which passed uneventfully and we soon settled down to squadron life. We were billeted about a mile from base, in the actual village of Marham, in a house known as Marham Hall, and the accommodation was one crew member per room. We walked to the base every morning to breakfast and returned to the house at about 6pm after tea, when we could do as we pleased. The weather grew warmer with the advent of spring and we used to kick a football around and generally muck about. Alex had a ukulele, which he played frequently, Bill somehow acquired a trombone, while I had a mouth organ. We formed a band and the noise we made was excruciating, but good fun.

Our gaiety was subdued one morning, when we were told by the crew in the next room that the bed of their second pilot was empty and still made up. We learned that, due to illness, he had been allocated to another crew for one trip and, while returning from this operation, they were forced to crash-land. He was assisting the skipper with the landing and, as he was not strapped in, he was flung forward on impact with the ground and was killed when his head struck the interior of the aircraft. He was the only casualty, but this incident shook us somewhat and brought home to us the precarious existence we were leading. However, this feeling was momentary and we simply rationalised the situation and carried on as naturally as we could. In fact we did what most combatants do, and regarded the event as always befalling the other chap.

In our leisure hours at weekends, if there were no ops, we took the bus to King's Lynn on Saturday evenings and, after a few drinks, we would usually end up in the local dance hall. We were invariably a trio of Bill,

Alex and myself. Geoff, who was recently married, and Bernie, who was of a sober disposition, kept their own company. Geoff was keen to have his wife living near the base, which we thought was a crazy idea, but, as he was determined, he, Bernie and I went searching for appropriate accommodation. We did find a suitable house but the lady owner was chary of letting it to aircrew owing to the uncertainty of our existence. In her own words: 'Unfortunately you young men are usually here today and gone tomorrow.' How right she proved to be. In Geoff's case, he did in fact agree to accept the lady's offer, but his poor wife never occupied the rooms for we were shot down before she was able to move in.

Daily life on the squadron was very laid-back. It started with our arrival at the flight hangar in the crew room, where we were given relevant information by our flight commander. We then dispersed to our respective aircraft to carry out daily inspections. In my case, I surveyed the guns and the hydraulics to ascertain whether the pressure was spot-on. I then checked the ammunition containers to ensure they were properly filled. We also examined the intercom system and the oxygen supply system. The rear turret, which I took over, was immaculately maintained and when I inspected the gun barrels, the rifling shone like silver.

The crew of our aircraft had just finished their tour of thirty trips and were on their way to various Operational Training Units as instructors. The former occupant of my rear turret was the recipient of the Distinguished Flying Medal. He preceded me at Lossiemouth and, while under training there, he was under threat of dismissal from the course, owing to his inability to master the theory and written exams. One day, on a training flight over the sea, the crew approached too close to the Norwegian coast and were attacked by a German fighter from Stavanger, which the rear gunner promptly shot down. He was awarded the DFM and nothing more was said about dismissal from training – hence his posting to Marham with his crew who had just completed their tour.

We also visited the parachute section and watched as the WAAFs expertly and deftly packed the parachutes with infinite care. This reminded me of one day, when I was ten years old, and I was eagerly reading my weekly tuppenny book, *The Wizard*, when I came upon an article entitled 'The Caterpillar Club', which described the origin and history of the use of parachutes for saving lives. I was an avid reader of anything pertaining to aviation and my imagination was fired by these tales of the life-saving properties of parachutes. So I went home, delved into the linen cupboard and found a discarded double-bed sheet, which was rather torn. I soon managed to repair the rents in the sheet and found a ball of binder twine, from which I cut four lengths, which I tied to the corners of the sheet. I decided there and then to try it out and, with two of my friends, excitedly made for the ruins of a Roman wall, which was about ten feet high. As I had no harness but merely the ends of the twine, I grabbed two ends in each hand and launched myself into space. The contrivance did partially break my fall, but not enough to prevent my landing in a crouching position and my knee making violent contact with my mouth, thus forcing one of my teeth through the flesh of my lower lip. I used the sheet to staunch the blood and made my way home, a much chastened would-be parachutist. Little did I dream that ten years hence, a real parachute would save my life.

One Saturday night, after the usual evening of boozing and dancing in King's Lynn, we made our way to the bus that was to take us back to camp. It was packed to the hilt with airmen, but with not a member of its driving crew in sight. We grew tired of waiting and suddenly Louis, an Argentinian pilot from the squadron, made his way to the driver's seat and proceeded to drive us back to base, some twelve miles distant. Upon arrival, we all melted into the night, leaving the bus to be collected by its rightful crew in the morning.[2]

The first of our four trips was to Emden and proved to be quite a tame affair. Our second 'op' was to Kiel and this was accomplished comfortably, despite the usual enemy efforts and the liberal use of heavy flak. Our third trip was to Brest, where we hoped to bomb the battleships *Scharnhorst* and *Gneisenau*. Due to the importance of the defence of this target, we were treated to a plentiful supply of flak of all calibres and I saw our bombs bursting on the dock infrastructure in close proximity to the two prime targets. Thanks to the skill of Bill, our observer, we succeeded on each trip in finding and bombing our target. Upon our return back to base after the Brest raid, we were treated to a sample of the Germans' latest ploy. They were following our aircraft home at a time when the crew would be congratulating themselves on another mission accomplished and then, as the British aircraft was flying straight and level on the approach for a landing, the enemy would place themselves immediately to the rear of the hapless bomber and easily destroy it with a few short bursts. The resulting losses from this activity were really serious as the stricken aircraft invariably hit the deck, with the loss of an aircraft and its crew.

We had just landed after the Brest raid and I had barely finished disrobing in the locker room, when an enemy aircraft flying low over the airfield deposited a stick of bombs across the runway and then disappeared into the night. They had obviously followed a landing aircraft but had not used their guns to destroy it. I always kept my guns armed and ready for action until we had rolled to a halt. The Germans used this intruder system throughout the war, and at the end of hostilities they had accounted for the loss of some hundreds of aircraft and crews.

Our fourth operation was the fateful final trip to Hamburg.

Chapter Three

Behind the Wire

After my period of solitary confinement at Dulag Luft, I was taken to a barrack hut where I joined some thirty fellow aircrew. We were at this centre for ten days, after which we left for the local railway station, and thence a journey to a prison camp. Our mode of travel was the usual cattle truck and there were thirty-nine of us aboard ours, together with six armed guards. We decided that during the journey we would escape by means of a train jump. The door of the truck was of the sliding variety, secured by a simple hook, which was on the outside and dropped into a U-bolt. When the door was closed, there remained a gap of about an inch – just enough room for a finger to flip up the bolt and shove the door back. We had assembled near the door and waited for the train to slow down on a suitable gradient. At an apt moment the bolt was raised, and the first five blokes exited immediately the door was shoved back.

I was number six in the queue and, as I sprang towards the door, the guard thrust his rifle and bayonet in front of me as a barrier and deterrent. By this time the train was travelling in a curve and I caught a glimpse of one of the escapees lying on the track after a bad landing. The guard also saw him and raised his rifle to fire, so I barged into him and knocked his rifle up. I had to act as though I had been pushed in the general turmoil, as the situation could have become highly dangerous had the guards started shooting indiscriminately. The train finally stopped and four of the guards jumped out with the intention of pursuing the escapers … then they all came back to collect their gas masks, which provoked roars of laughter from the prisoners. After about ten minutes they returned empty handed and we were herded to one end of the truck, while the guards occupied the other half. The NCO in charge of the guards was actually frothing at the mouth, and muttering incoherently, while all the time clicking the safety catch of his Schmeisser machine gun; it was somewhat unnerving until we became inured to the situation. In his mental state, he could so easily have shot us all, and claimed the reason as mass escape. We learned later that punishment for allowing POWs to escape was banishment to active service, which could mean serving on the Russian Front, with all of its attendant risks of death or captivity.

After a journey of some three or four days, we arrived at a town in Poland named Lodz. The Germans had renamed it as Litzmannstadt. We were housed in part of the university and a wire fence separated us from the other prisoners who, we learned, were the first Russian aircrew to be shot down when Germany invaded Russia. They were a cagey lot, and were loath to engage in conversation across the wire. However, we gained permission from the Germans to share our soup ration with them. One of our party spoke fluent French and he was able to induce our allies to accept the soup, which they did with an air of suspicion. There was never an aura of good fellowship or camaraderie between us, so we decided to leave them to their suspicious attitude.

Upon arrival at our sleeping quarters in the university building, we were allotted the usual two-tier wooden bunks, and I chose a top bunk. As I clambered up and crashed out on the straw palliasse, the small of my back encountered something very hard. I delved among the straw and discovered a lump of black bread the size of a half-brick. It was impossible to break, so I merely sucked and nibbled at it for several days until it disappeared.

One morning we were sitting outside in the June sunshine when I became aware of a movement in the long grass beyond the perimeter wire. Suddenly two small Polish boys leaped up and hurled a package in our direction. This contained some small cakes and a packet of cigarettes. As we were non-smokers, we shared these with three Russians who happened to be sitting near us. Next morning the same thing occurred, but the Russians collared the package and did not reciprocate our act of comradeship of the previous day. I thought, if that was communism, they could keep it.

As our accommodation was on the town's outskirts, we were not aware of what was happening in the town itself. It was after the war that we learned that part of the town was established as a Jewish ghetto, and the inhabitants were subjected to mindless cruelty and starvation, with people dropping dead in the streets. There were also mass movements of people to concentration camps, with a miserable death at the end of a terrible journey.

We remained at Lodz for two weeks, and then we were on the move again. Our destination was Stalag 18, at Wolfsberg in Austria, not far from Graz. We reached there one beautiful summer morning and we had to walk about two miles to the camp. The scenery was magnificent, with a backdrop of mountains wherever we looked. The camp was occupied by 18,000 French prisoners. We were allocated a barrack hut and once we were rested and revived, we set about cleaning the place until it met with our requirements. The ablution hut was in a dreadful state, with faeces and gobs of spittle everywhere. The whole place reeked of stale urine, and was still occupied by the French. We commandeered the building for our own use, and proceeded to clean it to British standards.

During our stay there, we experienced quite a number of spectacular thunderstorms, with brilliant lightning playing around the surrounding mountains. In due course we received our marching orders, and once again found ourselves boarding the inevitable cattle truck for an unknown destination. We were, in fact, en route to Stalag VIII-B at Lamsdorf, which was a German Army camp housing some 10,000 souls.

Upon our arrival we were allocated our own compound, which was solely for RAF prisoners, and I organised a group of keep-fit enthusiasts to form a physical training class. Within a week I had a class of thirty keen individuals, and we assembled daily for a workout. Soon after the formation of the class I was officially recognised as the Sports Führer and I received a regular weekly payment of lager geld (camp money). Of course, the money was only camp currency, and went into a communal fund, which enabled us to purchase soap and toothbrushes etc. as the need arose. I had my twenty-first birthday at this camp, at which point we were experiencing a particularly lean time, as Red Cross parcels were failing to arrive. We were existing on basic German rations comprising breakfast of ersatz coffee made with ground acorns and lunch, when the bread ration issued was a fifth of a loaf per man of rye bread, together with three or four boiled potatoes in their jackets, followed by a pint of watery soup, which contained the odd piece of swede floating about in it. Those were the daily rations and, owing to the low calorific value of the food, all sporting activities were suspended until the flow of Red Cross parcels was resumed.

It was on my twenty-first birthday that we heard the joyous news that Red Cross parcels had arrived! We entertained thoughts of a feast, but were hastily disillusioned when we learned that the consignment was one of tobacco parcels. The cigarette ration amounted to thirteen per man and, although I was a non-smoker, I thought that if I could not eat, I may as well smoke, and that was when I became a slave to the weed. The months passed, and winter arrived, and there were days when the temperature fell to twenty below zero. One day I touched the outside door handle and my fingers froze to the metal and I lost some skin when I tried to free them. The first Russian Army prisoners arrived, and many of them were partisans who had been captured at various regions of the Russian front. They were in a pitiful state, and they were really emaciated, their clothes hanging off their gaunt frames, looking like walking scarecrows.

They occupied the compound adjacent to ours. We organised some Red Cross tinned food for them, but as their numbers increased daily, our efforts were just a drop in the ocean. One evening, as a token of appreciation, they formed a choir near the wire that separated our compounds and sang for us. Their effort was magnificent and they seemed to have a natural propensity for choral singing, which touched us deeply. They received from the Germans a daily soup ration, which was obviously just a token. It was a deliberate German policy to starve them until they gradually died from this treatment. We did hear that there were cases of cannibalism among them.

One day, just after their soup ration arrived, the usual queue formed and the soup was being dished out when a commotion suddenly broke out and several shots rang out. We later learned that there was an argument about the soup ration and one of the German officers present shot a Russian. The Russian's mate then drew a bayonet from the scabbard of one of the German guards and ran it through the stomach of the officer, seized the officer's pistol and shot another of the guards. The

Russian was finally overpowered and he too was killed. This mayhem happened over a period of two minutes. The near riot was finally quelled, and the soup continued to be dished out.

We heard that working parties of Russians were digging large pits in nearby woods, and that they were to be used as mass graves. One morning I was on my way to the sick bay with a party of fellow sufferers (I had a badly sprained ankle) when an open lorry passed us. It seemed to be loaded with firewood in the form of white barkless branches. I then realised, with horror, that the load was skeletal corpses that had succumbed to the inhuman treatment received at the hands of their hosts. Naturally, their comrades had collared their clothing, such as it was, and they were on their way to their last resting places in the pits in the woods.

The Germans began to realise that they had bitten off more than they could chew on the Russian front, particularly with the growing shortage of oil and petrol, and the increasingly extended lines of communication. They were reduced to confiscating our flying boots, for reissue to their troops on the Russian front. I forestalled them by swapping mine for a rucksack, which I thought would be useful in the future.

The winter months dragged slowly by and in the spring we were ordered to make ready for a journey to a new RAF camp in Silesia, near the town of Sagan. This was Stalag Luft III; there were already prisoners from other camps who had been there some months before our arrival. The camp was highly organised, and the facilities for our welfare came as a welcome surprise after our nomadic wandering in the past. There was a library and a schoolroom, where people could study a wide range of subjects under the tutelage of qualified teachers. There was also a theatre where productions were regularly presented. There was even a camp orchestra, the instruments for which were supplied by the Red Cross and the YMCA from Geneva.

We had not been long at Sagan when there was an influx of people from another camp, and there among them was Alex Kerr, whom I had last seen lying wounded in a searchlight hut and, I had presumed, near death, but now looked very fit. Then, soon after our joyous reunion, Bill Legg arrived, which meant that, with the exception of Andy our skipper, who was sadly drowned when he bailed out and landed in the river, our complete crew was in the same camp. Bill and Alex had spent some time in hospital and Bill was recovering from an abdominal operation. When we were shot down he had sustained a bullet wound to the stomach while returning to his post after coming to help me with the fire in my turret. Of course, I knew nothing of this at the time. Neither was I aware that Bill had landed the aircraft. When he had returned to the front of the plane after he had seen me leave, he found that he was the only crew member aboard, so he decided to take over and attempt a landing. This he miraculously achieved, with the wheels up, after flying under some cable overhead, narrowly missing a row of houses and grinding to a halt not far from a hospital. By this time he was semi-conscious and he recollected being hacked out of the still burning aircraft by German troops and rushed to the adjacent hospital where an eminent French surgeon performed an immediate operation, which was fortunately successful. However, within a few months, Bill contracted dysentery and his stitches burst, thus destroying, irretrievably, the surgeon's work. The wound never healed, and Bill was repatriated to England in 1943.

With the advent of summer a group of air gunners, of which I was one, decided to start a tunnel. It was to be a mole job, which involved sinking a shaft near the warning wire and digging the tunnel in the direction of a new washhouse building which had recently been erected, but which was unused. Our plan was to achieve a supply of fresh air from the drainage system of this building, which would then enable us to continue beyond the main wire fence, and then to the point of evacuation in the trees beyond this boundary. The weather was warm and we made good progress with the sinking of the shaft. When we had attained a depth of six feet, we started the tunnel. All this work was executed under the judicious use of a blanket, which we rigged up on two sticks, ostensibly to shield us from the sun while sunbathing. The height of the blanket was sufficient to screen us from the attention of the guard in the watch-tower, and the shaft cover was constructed of bed boards. When the cover was in position it formed part of the small vegetable patch. We had to ensure that after each day's digging, the cover was replaced, and the lettuce plants on the cover remained fresh and in line with the existing rows in the plot.

The size of the tunnel was little more than the digger's body width, hence the 'moling' nature of the project. He relied on forward propulsion by the energetic use of elbows and toes, and the digger entered the tunnel with a rope attached to his ankle. He dug until he was near to passing out through lack of oxygen and then signalled his distress with two jerks of the rope, whereupon he was hauled out backwards and the next man took his place. Work proceeded steadily, and within two weeks we had reached the washhouse building.I happened to be the digger when the drain was reached and I had the task of breaking through the drain. I had to bang it several times before it shattered, and the result was a wonderful stream of fresh air, which enabled us to carry on digging for a further half-hour each, per shift.

We were aware that we would be unable to continue with the tunnel beyond the summer months, as we could hardly sunbathe in sunless conditions. We decided therefore to cease operations until the following summer. We reluctantly sealed the shaft and raked the soil of the plot over the cover, and fervently hoped that the half-completed building would remain in that state.

Shortly after we had abandoned the tunnel, the whole camp was agog with the prospect of another move to a camp at Heydekrug, near Königsberg. We had already begun prospecting for another tunnel, so we arranged with security that we should remain in the camp, ostensibly as permanent staff, when the exodus occurred. The compound was to be occupied by American officers, and they had already started arriving in large numbers, due to the extensive daylight bombing programme. We eventually decided on the site for the new tunnel, which involved creating a shaft in the main washhouse. Before we could start work on the excavation of the shaft, we had to break through the concrete base of the trap, which directed water to an adjacent soakaway, and form a trap cover which comprised a two-inch-thick slab of concrete on a base of boarding that had to fit the base of the trap and was removed and replaced during digging sessions. The waste water also had to be diverted slightly in order to avoid flooding the shaft.

The whole tunnel was to be boarded and an air provision system installed. The latter comprised a pump fashioned from a canvas kit bag supported in a wooden frame, and when completed it resembled a very large concertina. The air line consisted of dried milk tins, placed end on end, the ends having been removed, thus providing a tin air line. The pump operator sat and worked the bellows backwards and forwards in a rowing motion. The valves were made from the leather tongues of boots. The whole contrivance worked very efficiently and in no time we had many volunteers for the pumping job. In fact, within a very short period, we had an American colonel on each of the three shifts of three hours' duration. Work proceeded steadily and the summer weather remained dry and sunny, which was a boon, for after digging sessions we could have a shower, followed by sunbathing, during which we kept a sharp lookout for prowling ferrets (German special staff who paid us frequent visits, also referred to as goons). We organised a surveillance system so that immediately a goon entered the compound, his progress was charted and his every move checked until he finally left the area.

Roof falls were a constant cause for concern and, during one bout of digging, I heard a whoosh and thumping sound as I was engulfed in a heap of loose sand; my arms were pinioned to my sides and I was unable to move a muscle, with only my head visible above the heap. Fortunately, my digging mate was not affected by the fall and he was able to dig me out immediately. The whole experience was, however, extremely frightening and a salutary reminder of the dangers involved.

One day, during a sunbathing session, I saw a familiar figure approaching and although he was clad in a khaki battledress, I recognised him as Pilot Officer Alan McSweyn, our old skipper we had trained with in the Operational Training Unit in Scotland. He had changed identities with an Army private so that he would be able to join a working party outside and escape more easily than was possible from inside a camp. Alan invited me to join him in his bid for freedom, but as I was already committed to the tunnel project, I was obliged to decline his offer and we parted with mutual wishes of good luck.

This was in 1943 and Alan, along with a party of Army prisoners, was sent to an Army camp. Upon their arrival Alan spoke to the senior Army man and declared his intention of escaping, whereupon he was informed that there was a tunnel in the camp that extended beyond the wire and had been abandoned for some reason. Alan befriended a German-speaking Army man and, in due course, they used the tunnel and made their escape via the Pyrenees, although, due to the dreadful weather (it was then mid-winter), Alan's mate succumbed and died in the mountains. Before this, however, Alan spent some time with the French Maquis and he, as a pilot, was elected to survey and select sites suitable for light aircraft landing for the purpose of introducing SOE agents. Finally he arrived in England in 1944.

Meanwhile, the weather continued to favour us with its rainless and sunny state for several weeks, but then it started to rain and did not cease for over a week. We were all resting in our hut one day when the compound gates were hurriedly opened to admit a fire engine, which screeched to a halt near the washhouse, accompanied by much bellowing, and panic. By the time we had ambled over to see what was happening, a rescue operation was in hand. Due to the previous week's incessant rain, the soakaway, which serviced the washhouse, had given way and a slight depression had appeared. The soakaway measured some twenty feet by twenty feet by fifteen feet, and a prying German ferret had noticed the depression and had used his probe to examine it. The soakaway had caved in, taking him with it. The fire engine crew had managed to place a harness on the submerged ferret, and when we arrived on the scene, he was being hauled up from the morass, which was once the soakaway. Naturally, this gave rise to ironic cheers from us, at which the Germans took umbrage and loosed off a few rounds from their pistols. I have never in my life seen such a speedy evacuation as ensued, with people diving through open windows into their huts. Needless to say, that spelled the end of our tunnelling activities, as all our hard work had been demolished with a German fire hose.

However, we did start another tunnel from an unoccupied hut, with the excavation for the shaft situated beneath the heating stove at the end of the room. This involved a great deal of stove manhandling each time we worked on the shaft excavation. We had only made a small impression on the digging when we received orders to pack our kit and prepare to vacate the site. We were bound for the camp at Heydekrug, near Königsberg, which involved a journey of several days in the inevitable cattle trucks. This camp was the destination for the main body of people who had, some months ago, left Stalag Luft III, so it was a case of catching up with the main body of RAF Kriegies.

We had not been in our new surroundings for six months, when a request from the officers' camp at Barth, Stalag Luft I, for volunteers to act as batmen (servants) presented a great opportunity for an escape en route. There was a small number of aircraftmen in our camp who had been captured on Crete and they all volunteered for the job. Six of us asked to be included in the party as the opportunity to make a train break was too good to miss. We prepared our escape kit and, in particular, managed to acquire a couple of stout table knives, which had seen service in the German sentries' Mess hall. These we annealed with heat and, after forming a saw edge, they were re-hardened and – voila! – we had two saws for dealing with the cattle truck walls. It was our intention to leave the truck and head for Danzig, which was a busy port, and stow away on a Sweden-bound vessel.

As soon as we were allocated a truck we placed ourselves at one end and started to saw our way out. We were surprised at how efficient the saws were and aimed to cut out a square section of the truck side, measuring approximately two feet by two feet. After the first day's travelling we had the top and one side of the aperture sawn through. By the end of day two, we had completed the sawing and the panel was held by a mere half-inch of unsawn timber. We had planned to make our breakout during the small hours, when the train would be shunted into a siding and the sentries would, we calculated, be at their most inefficient. We had the addresses of two brothels in Danzig where previous escapees had received assistance from Polish people who, for obvious reasons, were not very kindly disposed towards the Germans.

The scheme was for a queue to form for the urine bucket at our end of the truck and under this cover, we would make our exit. We were contemplating a successful exit when the night was filled with shouts and shots, and the clamour of guttural shouts and the usual panic. It transpired that, despite our instructions that there should be no lone attempts, a guy from the adjoining truck had made a selfish solo exit. He was immediately re-captured, beaten up by the guards and left to suffer for his stupidity.

A thorough search of our truck by the guards revealed our escape hole and, for the remainder of our journey of five days, we were subjected to a rigorous regime of close surveillance and were herded together in the centre of the truck, which rendered any further escape attempts impossible. We eventually arrived at Barth, which housed RAF and American officer aircrew, and were allocated a hut adjacent to the American area of the camp. The hospitality of the Americans was overwhelming; they showered us with gifts of clothing, cigarettes and food from their Red Cross supplies, and we were accepted as unfortunate fellow downed flyers.

Regrettably, the same could not be said of our own officers, who appeared to be a stuffy lot of individuals. The day after arriving in camp, a bouncy little flying officer called at our hut and announced that we would not be required to start 'batting' until Monday, when we would be expected on parade at 09.00 hours. We politely informed him that senior NCOs did not 'bat' for anyone and that the reason we were here was due to an unsuccessful escape attempt. We were in the business of escaping, not acting as servants to officers. Subsequently, we were ordered to produce our escape equipment and to hand it over to the senior officer, but told him in no uncertain terms that our escape gear – compasses, maps and saws etc. – was our property and would remain so. Apparently the officers, owing to a lack of security, had lost nearly all of their escape kit during a recent search. We later learned that they placed more importance on trading with the Germans for the purposes of providing their Mess with 'goodies'.

On the Monday morning mentioned, only a few genuine batmen turned out for the parade – we just sat tight and awaited results. Sure enough, the same bouncy little FO arrived at our hut and announced that, owing to our attitude, we were to attend a court martial on the morrow, for failing to obey an order from a superior officer. We attended this farce as requested and there they all were, seated behind a long table, resplendent in what uniforms they could muster, ready to deal with us. Allowing them to do all the talking, we just stood in front of them, looking blasé and not saying a word. They then reduced each one of us to the ranks. I suppose the thought was that, having reduced us to the lowest possible rank, we would have to obey them and act as servants in our new capacity. They could not have been more mistaken, for we simply walked back to our quarters and carried on as if this stupid farce had never happened.

We then organised a band of American officers and started a tunnel near the boundary wire. We were making good progress when, after a few weeks, we were told that we would be returning to our own camp at

Heydekrug. So, once again, we packed our bags and set off. There were twelve of us in the returning party and, as we were regarded as determined escapers, we were favoured by the attendance of eight heavily armed guards. Upon arrival at the station, there was a mile or two hike to the camp. I was walking next to my friend Tony O'Brien, a captured member of the 1st SAS. Within earshot of the English-speaking guard commander, as a joke, he said to me: 'You take the guard on the right and I'll take the one on the left.' The guard commander promptly issued an order to his troops, whereupon they moved several paces away from us. As if we would have tried anything so senseless with such a heavily armed bunch.

When we arrived at the camp we learned that, in our absence, an escape had been made. Several blokes had made a successful exit, but they had all been recaptured and were in the cooler (solitary confinement). When the tunnel was discovered, the Germans went mad and ordered everyone outside, while they searched the rest of the huts for other possible tunnels. Naturally, the inmates milled about and an attempt by the Germans to organise a roll-call met with scant success. They then produced two long ladders, which they placed side-by-side, tapering at one end to a gap of two feet. They then positioned a table at the tapered end, the idea being to have all the men's dossiers in neat piles on the table so that they could drive the Kriegies slowly through the gap and check each man's credentials in an orderly manner as they passed through. The procedure got under way and someone began bleating like a sheep; then the whole assembly started to bleat and pandemonium followed. There was a stampede towards the table, which was overturned with all the documents scattered to the four winds. People grabbed the papers and distributed them among the crowd. Not much remained of the original neat pile – they were either burned or stuffed down the latrine. For several weeks anyone whose dossier was missing spent two weeks in the cooler.

Eventually, things settled down and summer arrived. We had received some cricket gear via the Red Cross and we organised a series of games between various representative teams. We had test matches, England v Australia, and some other matches, such as south of England v MCC, north of England v MCC and so on. For some time we had been aware of the noise of heavy gunfire and the general rumble of artillery as the Russian front moved towards us and, during a match between south of

England and MCC, I was batting for the former, when the camp guards invaded the pitch and ordered us to pack up as the whole camp was moving to Thorn in Poland. We reluctantly abandoned the game and proceeded to pack our scant belongings in preparation for the exodus.

I grabbed a brand new cricket bat for future use, if we ever got the chance. However, one of the guards ordered me to surrender the bat, on the grounds that it could be used as a weapon. We vacated the camp and had to march a couple of miles to the railway station, but were allowed a short rest at the halfway mark, which was at a small village. A crowd of villagers gathered outside their houses to watch the Tommy prisoners and one kindly woman sent her toddler son out to us with a large jug of water, which he could hardly carry. He was a lovely looking little chap, with straw-coloured hair and blue eyes and he was wearing a vibrant one-piece cotton summer suit. As he approached us, one of the guards knocked the jug from the little fellow's hands and then set his Alsatian dog on the infant, who was bitten. There were loud cries of protest from us, and things could have become ugly if we had not been moved on. One of our chaps was bayoneted in the rump and he marched on, bleeding profusely. We finally boarded the train and arrived at our destination in the early hours of the next morning, following another two-mile walk from the station.

This was an Army camp, housing some 10,000 men and was fully organised in true British Army style. As soon as we arrived, in an exhausted condition, the cookhouse was opened up and we were given large mugs of steaming hot, sweet tea, which to this day remains the finest pick-me-up I have ever experienced. The camp seemed to have an adequate supply of Red Cross food parcels and, as the days and weeks progressed, we were restored to physical fitness – so much so, that we were able to challenge the Army team to a game of rugger. We began training as the opposition and, with 10,000 troops to choose from, were able to muster a very strong fifteen. The Army finally posted their team on the camp noticeboard, and it was laced with several international players.

About a week before the date of the game, I was walking round the compound when, in the distance, at the main gate, I saw a fresh intake of prisoners arriving. They were all in Army khaki uniforms and wore slouch hats. Some of them were physically enormous and we later learned that they were South African troops who had been captured at Tobruk, in the Middle East. Two or three days later, we were passing the Army noticeboard and stopped to read it. Much to our surprise, the original team had been changed and now included some South African names, including six players from the 1939 international Springbok pack, as well as a sprinkling of internationals in other positions.

The day of the match arrived and we lined up for the start, looking like a team of pygmies against a team of giants. It was a tough game and we were determined to put up a good show, so we got stuck in – the end result was a victory for the Army of twenty-one points to three.

We had been at this camp for three months when we had orders to prepare for yet another move, this time to a place called Fallingbostel, a camp primarily for RAF prisoners. We settled down to the routine of camp life, which was often pleasantly enlivened by large formations of American aircraft on their way to create havoc on some luckless town. On one particular occasion we were all outside cheering as the bombers passed overhead, when we were ordered by the camp guards to end our jubilation and assemble for roll-call. Despite the angry yells of the guards, I continued to cheer on the USA aircraft until I realised that I was on my own and was being approached by a guard who spoke excellent English and was in fact one of the camp interpreters. I quickly made off and attempted to hide in our barrack hut, but he pursued and finally cornered me, so I had no choice but to surrender. He asked me my name and number, and I replied Whitehall No. 1212. I was in the process of reading a detective novel about Scotland Yard and its telephone number featured in the story. I then joined the rest of the prisoners on roll-call while my erstwhile pursuer approached the German officer taking the parade and 'Herr Whitehall' was requested to step forward and identify himself. I stood firm, but following threats by the Germans to withhold all privileges and a prolonged roll-call for the whole camp, I surrendered and was sentenced to a week in the cooler.

I was allowed to take one book with me so chose Dickens's *Pickwick Papers*, which I hoped would last me the whole week. However, in the circumstances, this proved to be an unsuitable choice. The frequent descriptions of numerous stagecoach journeys, laced with their consequent stops, during which there were detailed accounts of the gargantuan meals enjoyed by the travellers, were agonising. As I was subsisting on the scant prisoners' rations, I suffered unbearable pangs of food deprivation, so I abandoned the book.

While in the cooler I was permitted to exercise every morning by walking around a well-trodden track on an extremely small area of land. There was a spyhole in the door of my cell and I was aware of the frequent use of this by the guard. The meals were very basic and comprised a thick slice of black bread each day, washed down with some form of coffee made from ground acorns or some other substitute. At lunchtime there was a bowl of watery soup containing particles of swede with the odd strand of cabbage floating about in it. Once, during the week, I was given a pat of margarine and a spoonful of some sort of jam. My cell was not far from the German barracks, and I could hear the strains of Wagnerian music for most of the day. The music sounded jubilant and victorious. Perhaps they were attempting to buoy their spirits, as they must have been aware of the rapid advance of our troops.

Chapter Four

Beyond the Wire

One morning in April 1945, we were informed that we would have to vacate the camp and go on the march, destination unknown. By this time I had teamed up with John Egan, a bomber pilot, Gerry Clark, a spitfire pilot, Ron Chisholm, an American who had joined the RAF as an air gunner, and Jock Bell, who had been a member of the RAF Regiment and was captured on Crete. We decided that if we marched, we would be at the mercy of the Germans, who might become involved in our being used as hostages. The camp guards started to round us up for the proposed trek, so we made ourselves scarce by hiding in several places until the tumult and the shouting had died away. Then, seizing our opportunity, we made for the wire and discovered a small hole, which we soon enlarged, and broke through to freedom.

Once outside, the feeling of freedom was overwhelmingly intoxicating and we could hardly believe that, after so many abortive attempts at digging for freedom, we were actually outside the wire. We made tracks in the direction of the front line and, at one stage we heard a very adjacent blast, which came from a mortar that some enemy troops were operating in a nearby orchard. Then, further on, we saw other troops mining a culvert. Later, we came upon a battery of guns in a large clearing in a wood. Far from being used to stem any attacks by the advancing Allied troops, there was complete and utter panic, as everyone at the position seemed bent on making their escape. There were officers, two up on motorcycles, charging away in an easterly direction, and we did not remain long enough to discover whether the troops had spiked the guns.

Shortly after witnessing this debacle we came upon a farmhouse, so decided to call there for some refreshment. On entering by the back door into the kitchen we found seated at a long, typical farmhouse table the farmer's wife and six German soldiers, who had obviously deserted and wanted nothing more to do with the war. We stayed there for an hour, having eaten a very light lunch of the usual black bread and some ersatz coffee, then pressed on.

While crossing an area of heathland we spotted a tank approaching. It stopped about eighty yards in front of us and trained its gun in our direction. A black-bereted head appeared out of the conning tower and we yelled, 'Don't fire, we're English.' The tank then edged up and stopped, and some of the crew dismounted and handed round some cigarettes. So there we were, with the odd shell whistling overhead, enjoying a smoke beside a British Cromwell tank. We informed the crew about the German mining party and they subsequently dealt with the mines.

We also told them about the Germans at the farmhouse. The squadron commander was Major Hepburn, whom the troops referred to as 'Kathy'. He sent up an armed party to investigate the farmhouse. The corporal in charge was an Austrian who had joined the Army after reaching England, following the Germans taking over his native country. We were with the 8th Hussars of the 7th Armoured Division. Within twenty minutes, a body of troops approached from the direction of the farm and when they arrived there were the six Germans we had seen at the farm, plus twenty other enemy soldiers who had been hiding in the cowshed when we were there. Major Hepburn lined them up in front of us and ordered them to place the contents of their rucksacks in front of them. The rucksacks were stuffed full of cigars, cigarettes, large tins of meat and bottles of eau de cologne. We were invited to take what we wanted, which we did with great alacrity before having a meal with the troops, and were most impressed by some strange white stuff, which was bread baked by the Army, no doubt.

As we ate, the news on the tank's radio informed us that President Roosevelt's life was gradually ebbing away; he died later that evening, 12 April 1945. We were then armed by the tank crew with rifles and yards of .303 ammunition with which to protect ourselves. This was deemed necessary, as there were pockets of German troops still holding out, even though they had been overrun during our advance. They were invariably

SS troops who had a reputation for dying hard, and were not particular who they took with them. We were fortunate not to have encountered these troops as, with their superior fire power, we would not have survived.

Boarding a jeep we were driven for several miles to Div ACK, in a small town, coming to a halt in the town square where we were immediately surrounded by a milling crowd of civilians who indicated by sign language that they were very hungry. Realising they were liberated inmates from a nearby concentration camp, we promptly doled out all the food that we had taken from the Germans. Their faces, which bore the unmistakeable signs of starvation, lit up in anticipation of a feast.

We took our leave of the jeep and the driver went on to his destination. Setting out to leave the town, after a couple of miles we came upon a small airfield and a tented camp. This was occupied by an Army Co-op squadron of Auster aircraft, which were used for artillery spotting. Making ourselves known to the occupants, who were most welcoming, we had a shower and were given a meal, followed by the provision of a bed in a vacant tent. We were amazed to find that all the tents in the camp were extremely well furnished, with sumptuous armchairs and settees, all of which had been liberated from a large German house nearby, formerly owned and occupied by a prominent Nazi official. The bed linen was also 'liberated' and the next morning we awoke to the shout of 'looting party up'. A jeep and three bods roared off to the mansion for a further supply of bed linen. This invariably happened whenever the bed linen required changing. We never did find out whether there were any laundry facilities.

After this good night's rest, we took to the road the following morning. Whenever we felt hungry or thirsty, we simply presented ourselves to the nearest convenient Army unit, where we were usually refreshed and re-victualled. With our rifles and the ammunition wound about us in the form of bandoliers, we must have presented a highly irregular picture, and had many strange looks from the occupants of passing staff cars advancing with our attacking troops.

The weather was gloriously spring-like and warm even if the dust raised by armoured cars and tanks rendered visibility nil at times. We witnessed one glorious sight as a squadron of the Guards Armoured Division roared past, only just discernible in the dust haze. As the day wore on we were wondering where we were going to spend that night, when we saw four RAF airmen approaching, so asked them where they were from. They informed us that they were with a transport command unit, but only a couple of miles away there was a 2nd Tactical Air Force unit flying Typhoons and Tempests. We opted for the latter and made our way in the indicated direction until arriving at an aerodrome resembling a scrapheap. There were wrecked German aircraft lying around everywhere. The runway was clear, however, and we noticed several Typhoons dispersed about the place.

On approaching the entrance gates we were challenged by the sentry, who barred our progress and called for the guard to turn out. Handing in our weapons we were then interrogated by the unit's security officer, who subsequently issued us with passes stating that we were escaped POWs. Given accommodation and a hot shower, we were also invited to the Officers' Mess for dinner. After the meal we repaired to the bar where there was a plentiful supply of all kinds of liquor and cigarettes. It transpired that we were the guests of 122 Wing, 2nd TAF. The CO was Group Captain Jameson, who had only recently taken over the airfield during the rapid advance of our troops. As we entered the anteroom there was a group of pilots drinking at the bar. One of them suddenly left the bar and rushed over to Gerry Clark and embraced him. It was Gerry's former flight commander at Biggin Hill, Pierre Closterman no less, a recognised air ace who, after the war, became a French MP and wrote two very successful books. He was a flamboyant character and always wore a couple of pistols like a gun-slinging cowboy.

As the evening wore on, the alcohol flowed freely but, strangely, we remained unaffected by the amount consumed. Not so Jimmy Jameson who, while seated at a table, gradually subsided under it and finished in a heap. But we were still quite sober and I can only attribute our state to an almost total absence of alcohol during our incarceration in Germany. There was elation the next morning when the squadron security officer informed us that we would be able to fly back to Dunsfold, in Surrey, in a transport aircraft. However, when Movement Control was informed of our intentions, they insisted that we travelled under their jurisdiction, through the official channels. This we did, and were duly kitted out in brand new khaki battledress uniforms.

We eventually ended up at Brussels Airport. The whole place was humming with activity as aircraft landed and departed continuously. They were flying jerry cans of petrol in, then loading up with POWs and flying back to England; it was a veritable merry-go-round. When our aircraft arrived it was a Stirling bomber and, in due course, we boarded and were finally off back to dear old England.

When I mentioned in a conversation with the skipper that I was a rear gunner, I was allowed to occupy the rear turret for the trip home, with a lump in my throat and the prospect of soon seeing the English coast appearing. We eventually landed at Wing and our welcome there was beyond belief and extremely emotional. The personnel could not do enough for us and I am sure that most of the station's staff had volunteered to participate in the proceedings.

The meal provided was astronomical and comprised a huge variety of sandwiches and an enormous range of cakes. After this feast we were duly transported to RAF Cosford in Staffordshire, from where we would ultimately be sent home on indefinite leave. We arrived at Cosford on a Saturday evening so had the whole of Sunday to prepare for a rigorous day on Monday.

On Monday morning we awoke relaxed and fresh after a good night's rest, and able to face with equanimity whatever came our way. Firstly, we were kitted out in brand new RAF battledress to replace the khaki gear we had arrived in. Then there was a debriefing, during which we had to give a written account of our being shot down. This was followed by a really stringent medical examination. Finally, we were paid an amount of cash and provided with travel warrants to our respective homes.

Chapter Five

After the Wire and After the War

In the period of leave that followed I used to spend my time in central London, travelling up from home (the south-east suburbs) every morning and meeting former POW friends for a pub crawl. In those days you could not walk a hundred yards without meeting somebody you knew. On one occasion, while returning home, I fell asleep on the train and awoke somewhere in Kent and then had to make my way back on various trains, arriving home in the small hours.

This way of life continued until early June 1945 when I was posted to RAF Wittering in Huntingdonshire on the A1. I arrived in the early evening and freshened up with a shower. When I returned to my room I was greeted by two ex-POWs from the next room who had preceded me by a week. Although I had decided on a quiet evening of relaxation, my two neighbours appeared to be preparing for a night out. They informed me that this was the night of the station dance, which was held in a hangar with a bar in one corner. I elected to follow their example, especially as they mentioned that around 8pm a party of WAAFs from a secret radio station would arrive to enliven the proceedings.

The dance was very well attended and I took up a position at the bar, quietly sipping a pint. Sure enough, just after 8 o'clock the door burst open and a gaggle of about a dozen WAAFs trooped in. I carried on drinking until I was aware that the music had stopped and the MC was announcing the next dance, which was a Hokey Cokey. Looking around at the seated new arrivals I immediately noticed a small chestnut-haired girl who seemed to be unattached. I asked her to dance and she accepted my invitation. She was a lively girl and a natural conversationalist and we seemed to be mutually attracted. Her name was Barbara and we spent the rest of the evening together until her transport arrived. This was a jeep driven by her escort, a balding squadron leader who seemed not a little displeased at having been dumped that evening.

I could not stop thinking of Barbara. The next morning I phoned her and made a date for the following day. She was a radar operator and she and her colleagues worked a three-watch system, which allowed them to have one day free until 5pm. The next day was glorious weather, so I mounted my bike and pedalled away to see my new-found friend. We had arranged to meet at The Bell, an old pub frequented by the RAF at Market Deeping. Barbara was off duty all day and, with several of her colleagues, we seated ourselves at a long trestle table to eat al fresco. The landlady, Mrs Smith, was a first-class cook and catered for fishermen. Our table was soon laden with lots of lovely food, as any surplus of what she had cooked for the fishermen found its way on to our plates. So there I was, sitting in the sun in the pub garden, at a table with a bevy of lovely girls. We rounded off the meal with a basket of strawberries and a plentiful supply of cherries. The conversation flowed, interspersed with the usual cheerful banter, liberally spiked with humour and the atmosphere was one of great comradeship and esprit de corps enjoyed by all present. Following the meal we set out for the local gravel pit where we sunbathed and swam for the rest of the afternoon, until the girls had to be on duty that evening. I cycled the fourteen miles back to camp, a deliriously happy man who was madly in love with his WAAF. Yes, it had been a case of love at first sight.

After a four-month courtship, Barbara became my wife in October 1945. Following a short honeymoon in the Lake District, we began our married life at Red Lodge in Tunbridge Wells, living with Barbara's parents. I was successful in obtaining a government grant under the Further Education and Training Scheme to enable me to train as a pupil Chartered Surveyor, while Barbara contemplated her future with a watchful eye.

We continued living with her parents while I took a post as a pupil surveyor with a local firm of surveyors and auctioneers, until my principal managed to secure for me a new timber-framed bungalow. Then Barbara's father bought us a woodland site for conversion to a building site in Petteridge, East Sussex. Like true pioneers, we cleared enough of the woodland ourselves to accommodate the house, which was soon erected, for a budding chartered surveyor and a practical down-to-earth housewife, both eager to make our marks on local society and to bring up a family.

What with house-building and raising a family (our first-born, Alison, came along in the spring of 1947), I never did get round to passing the exams and decided to seek a situation that would provide a more substantial income. I landed a job as a sales representative with Sharps, the celebrated confectionery manufacturers. Alas, this meant leaving our much-loved woodland home and living in Nottinghamshire. We moved into a period cottage in a small village called Upton, near Newark, by which time we had added to our family with Joanna, our second daughter.

By the late 1950s I decided it was high time that I sought a job in which my recently acquired experience of salesmanship could marry up with the technical knowledge gained during my studies for professional qualifications in surveying. I secured a post with a Midlands-based manufacturer of concrete frame industrial farm buildings and, to my great joy, my territory was to be the county of Cornwall. It had always been an ambition of mine to live and work in Cornwall, and so, in 1960, we departed for the Duchy – now a family of five with the addition of my son, Stephen.

A large house overlooking St Austell Bay became our beloved family home and a life lived by the sea provided us with the opportunity to pursue the energising and invigorating sport of surfing. This was a year-round pursuit for us, not just in Cornwall but also on the Continent, and was something I continued to enjoy until I reached the grand old age of eighty, whereupon I sold my surfboard and bought a brand new continental hybrid bike that converted to a cross-country bike with a simple change of wheels. In this way I have managed to maintain a level of fitness beyond the age of ninety.

I marvelled at the way Barbara and I usually disagreed about most things, but our arguments were carried out quietly and with conviction. But the bedrock of our long and loving marriage was a solid belief and total agreement on important matters, in which category were included the children's welfare and their future and a total disregard for the lack of money to indulge in luxury. Also, unlike some ambitious types, I refused to allow my work to intrude into the family well-being.

I was not a 'company man' and I regarded my job simply as a means of providing a decent standard of living for the family. Even so, I enjoyed, and took great pride in, my occupation and there was never ever a Monday morning feeling. Furthermore, the results of my labours were spread over three counties and still exist today, as monuments to an enjoyable working life. But all good things come to an end and we were forced to leave Cornwall when the Midlands agency I worked for decided to curtail their activity in the West Country, despite my years of successful sales. Given the lack of specialist job opportunities in Cornwall and the reduced economic circumstances we found ourselves in, we had no choice but to return to the south-east where Barbara's family had a holiday cottage at Winchelsea Beach. We bought out the other family members and improved and extended the property and I began another career as a freelance gardener. So Winchelsea became our home (although we did retain ownership of a small cottage on the north coast of Cornwall and visited whenever we could) and is where I still live – with my daughters and most of my grandchildren and great grandchildren nearby. Stephen and his wife emigrated to Australia, but we have enjoyed many visits over the years, not only to catch up with nearest and dearest, but also to visit Alex, second pilot on the fateful night we were shot down.

Meeting up with Alex was on the agenda the very first time we travelled across the world to see our son in the 1970s when they were living in Sydney. After a wonderful family Christmas and New Year, we flew to Perth to call in on Alex, whom I had not seen for more than thirty years. I wondered how he had fared physically and, when he and his wife Joan met us at the airport, I was glad to see that he was still remarkably fit and very active. He had retired from his post as deputy chancellor at Murdoch University and was engaged in various financial schemes using his knowledge of economics to advantage. Our days with Alex and Joan were so enjoyable and consisted of early morning rounds on the golf course, fishing trips on Alex's motorboat and evenings of piano music (Joan was an accomplished pianist) and twilight drinks and dinners in the back garden, half of which was a swimming pool. We also became well acquainted with Alex's larger-than-life friend Nobby Clarke, who was an ex-Spitfire pilot who spent much of his service fighting the Japanese

Air Force. He was a great character, full of stories and adventures with which he would regale us until we were all splitting our sides with helpless laughter.

On our second trip to Australia we visited Alan McSweyn, our original pilot from our training course days. He and his wife Barbara lived in Queensland in a very pleasant waterside suburb where everybody seemed to have a motorboat moored outside their front door. When Alan had arrived in England in 1943 after his escape from Germany, he had married Barbara who was in the RAF as a code and cipher officer, and after the war they had settled in Australia, Alan's home territory. For several years Alan flew for Qantas, the leading Australian airline, and when he retired he and Barbara set up house in Queensland.

After a fine few days with them – the incredible heat made bearable by cooling trips on the motorboat and tours of the area in the comfort of an air-conditioned car (a luxury unknown in England) – we moved on to stay again with Alex and Joan for the New Year. They laid on a big party at which I met a fellow former POW, a New Zealander who was farming in New Zealand and with whom we had some common acquaintances, including Johnny Bulford, who had worked on our big tunnel in the POW camp, and I said that Johnny was now a farmer. They were all hugely surprised that Johnny was farming because, as far as they knew, he was living in Oxford. I informed him that Johnny was indeed at Oxford where he had obtained a degree in Land Agency and Estate Management as his family had over a thousand acres in Oxfordshire to manage! The party lasted well into the small hours and, like the time before at Alex's, we conjured up marvellous memories that will last for as long as we are alive.

Alex and Joan also came to the UK to see us and even accompanied us to France one year for a holiday. On this occasion we visited the beaches that our troops had invaded on D-Day, 6 June 1944. We spent the morning marvelling at the achievements of the Allied troops who took part in the operation to dislodge the enemy from its coastal strongholds and enable them to thrust forward into France. Alex and I also discovered a huge museum, displaying every kind of exhibit relating to the war. We spent two hours there and then went to meet the girls, who had prepared a visit to the Bayeux Tapestry. When we returned to our accommodation in the evening the French lady who owned the farm and gite we had rented invited us into her house for drinks and we swapped yarns about the war days and the experience of occupation by the enemy. When I mentioned that I had met Pierre Clostermann, the celebrated French flying ace, she told me that her son and Pierre's son were colleagues, flying helicopters for the French police force.

It was a wonderful holiday and the precursor to another three-week jaunt around France and Spain together. Revelling in stories of the war at our lodgings in the foothills of the Pyrenees one evening, we were overheard and introduced to a French local, a real character, who regaled us with stories of his wartime exploits as a guide for evading airmen and escaped prisoners of war. His descriptions of the risks taken were quite hair-raising; he was shot at many times and showed us the scar on his ear from a bullet that had whizzed by his head. Before our party broke up, Alex went to his room to fetch the tie he had recently received from the 'Escape Society' in London and presented this coveted prize to the Frenchman as a gift. Needless to say, our newfound friend was totally overwhelmed. We found out in the morning when preparing to leave and settle up that he had insisted on paying the bill for our dinner.

Wartime experiences undoubtedly cement lifelong friendships, but there came about another interesting reunion fifty years after we had been shot down.

In 1989 a Canadian tourist was on holiday in Germany and, while browsing in a junk shop in Hamburg, he came across a photograph album. As he idly flipped through the pages, he noticed a snapshot of a crashed Wellington bomber. Thinking of his friend (and also the local postman) Steve Martin back home in Canada, who was an avid collector of Second World War memorabilia, he bought the album as a gift.

On his return home, he presented a delighted Steve with the album. When Steve examined the shot of the Wellington more closely, he noticed that the registration number of the aircraft was visible – and so contacted the Air Ministry in London, who were most helpful and supplied him with further details of the aircraft, including the names of the crew members. The civilian archivist to the squadron, Don Bruce, lived only eight miles from us, but I was unaware of his existence. He proceeded to comb his local telephone directory until he found my name as one of the crew and rang me. He acquainted me with the details of the enquiry and we became great friends, especially as he told me that he was a former member of No. 115 Squadron, flew as a bomb aimer and was shot down in 1942 when he became a POW. I was able to furnish him with the names and addresses of my former crew mates who were still living. He also put me in touch with postman Steve in Canada and I was able to give him all the relevant information he required for his dossier.

Following on from that, we were all interviewed by the press in our respective localities, and the spread of the news eventually resulted in a reunion none of us had dreamed of. It was arranged for the surviving members of the crew – Bill Legg, Geoff Hogg and I – to fly to Germany in May 1991 to meet the pilot who had shot us down. Bill's son-in-law, a commander in the Fleet Air Arm and a helicopter pilot, had been working with NATO and liaising with German aircrew. He was able to organise this special trip to meet the German pilot, Hauptman Eckhart Wilhelm von Bonin, on the fiftieth anniversary of our downing.

On the appointed day we took off from RAF Benson in Oxfordshire in a Heron, an obsolescent aircraft, which was formerly part of the Queen's Flight. We arrived at our destination in the late afternoon and were standing near our aircraft when we were aware of a lonely figure leaning against a motor car on one of the approach roads. He came towards us and introduced himself as von Bonin.

There was not the slightest feeling of animosity and he was regarded in the same light as any other ex-member of aircrew, British or German. He said he was deeply touched by Bill's condition and he apologised for having wounded him. He also told us that we were his first victims and that, in the excitement of the engagement, he had forgotten to arm his cannon and fired only his machine guns. Had he used his cannon, we would probably not have been alive today.

We were accommodated in the officers' quarters and, when we weren't dining out, we ate in the Officers' Mess. On the first night we strolled over to the Mess and as Bill found it difficult to walk, von Bonin gave him a lift in his car. On the way they struck a kerb and then nudged another obstacle, causing Bill to remark that our host was a bloody awful driver. Jokingly he said to von Bonin: 'You tried to kill me fifty years ago and now you are at it again!' This provoked hoots of laughter and the evening that followed was one of good fellowship and merriment as the beer flowed until the late hours.

The next day we were provided with a people-carrier type of vehicle and a driver and went in search of the actual site of Bill's crash-landing. We had almost given up hope of ever finding the location when we passed a house where a man was painting at the top of a ladder. He descended as we stopped and told him of our quest and excitedly he exclaimed that he was only nine years of age at the time, but he could show us exactly where the stricken aircraft had landed, not far from his house. He guided us to the site and we had our photographs taken. It was a moving occasion as we contemplated the events of that night, fifty years before. We dined out that evening and the atmosphere in the restaurant was charged with goodwill and bonhomie. Von Bonin was a great trencherman and devoured huge steaks and all that was placed before him. I chided him about his appetite and warned him of the strain he was placing on his heart but he laughingly said that 'fleisch ist gut' and he thrived on it. Sadly he died with heart trouble the following January. The Canadian postman, Steve, remained in touch with von Bonin's wife and, as he was engaged in writing a biography of her husband, she made a present to him of von Bonin's Ritterkreuz (Knight's Cross) and other decorations.

Afterword

Anyone reading these memoirs might be inclined to think that as prisoners of war we spent all our time digging tunnels but, although escape was a prime factor in our thoughts, there were other outlets for our energy. I was a member of the camp choir and we also formed three quartets, performing Handel's Messiah; the experience of singing in a large choir with full orchestra, feeling the power generated, was a unique feature in camp life. I was chosen to take the role of Nanki Poo in Gilbert and Sullivan's *The Mikado*. We rehearsed most days, and our standards improved as time went on. However, on each occasion when we were ready to produce the show, we had to move camp and start again. This happened several times, until our final marching orders materialised, so I had to abandon the score, which I had carried all over Germany in my rucksack.

We also had a good library and there were classes conducted by qualified teachers in a wide range of subjects. Most importantly, we were able to engage in sporting activities, mainly rugger and soccer. I played a great deal of rugger, when my back wasn't giving me trouble, and, as the various teams comprised players of all nations, I gained greatly from their attitudes to the game and their robust tactics.

There were occasions when I was beset with general depression and the worst bout of this was in 1943 when we seemed to be losing the war on all fronts. A veritable black mental cloud descended and rendered me useless and apathetic with no will to either think of, or do, anything. I felt that I could so easily have walked towards the wire until the fatal shot would have solved my problems. However, after a few days suffering, I was mentally restored and thankfully I never experienced the feeling again.

I was shot down as a brash young man and, during the final days of my captivity, I felt that I would emerge a better and much wiser person. So, by and large, and as with rugger, mixing with all types and nationalities, I benefited hugely intellectually, and was more mentally equipped to face the outside world.

1	2	3	4	5	6	6	7	8	9	10	11	12	13	14	1

Name:

Albert Gunn

Bomber Command Air Gunner
Failed to Return from a 29/30 December 1943 Raid to Berlin

Chapter Six

A Tremendous Fascination

Like many young people of that period, the war proved to have a tremendous fascination, and I remember coming out of the Rialto cinema in Kirkaldy and walking into the Royal Air Force recruiting office and volunteering. I had just celebrated my eighteenth birthday. I was called to Edinburgh where I had all the various medicals, tests and interviews before being accepted for pilot training. I was then told I may have to wait for some eighteen months before call-up, but should I volunteer as an air gunner I would be called up much quicker and would be remustered later for pilot training when my turn came up – how easily we were conned! I duly accepted and returned home to find that my call-up papers for the Army had arrived that day in the post, so luckily I avoided having to wear a kilt with the Argyll and Sutherland Highlanders.

I eventually received my call-up papers for the RAF and was ordered to report to Lord's Cricket Ground, St John's Wood, London, which was the reception centre for RAF aircrew, and for the first time I left Scotland on the night train to King's Cross and duly reported on 15 March 1943. I still have clear recollections of my first meal at Lord's, sitting on the sloping grass bank, leaning against the pavilion railings, the view seen many times since on television as batsmen leave or return to the pavilion.

We were divided into flights of thirty men and allocated billets in Abbots Close, St John's Wood, luxury flats that had been requisitioned by the RAF, and so began our initiation into service life. Each flight was in the charge of a corporal who started the day by ringing the fire bell on the ground floor at 6am and then running up the stairs, and anyone found in contact with his bed had his name taken and was then punished, usually by being sent to the cookhouse to assist in the washing up in the evening. We learned quickly that we were a source of cheap labour, and it then became a battle of wits between the flights and the corporals. I was caught only once for leaving the cookhouse without wearing my hat and spent the next evening serving my sentence. The food did not seem so appetising after seeing the way some of it was prepared.

We were kitted out with uniforms, but were not allowed to wear them for the first week, as we were not considered fit persons to do so, and we were astonished at the care taken to ensure our uniforms fitted. Many were sent back to the tailor for adjustment. Much energy was expended in the evening polishing buttons and belts, but more particularly on the service boots with which we had been issued.

Our days were fully occupied with lectures and drilling; everywhere we went we had to march as a flight. Lectures were given in the Seymour Halls, and swimming in the Seymour Baths. The swimming aptitude test was fairly simple. All had to strip naked and were lined up at one end of the pool, when an invitation was given to anyone who could swim a length to carry on, then anyone who could swim a width were requested to oblige, until only the unfortunate non-swimmers were left. Many improved their swimming abilities dramatically as the balcony surrounding the pool was lined by WAAF office staff and the longer one waited the more 'exposed' one became (and more embarrassed). I think I was one of the first to finish a length of the pool and escape back to the dressing room. Our only return to Lord's was for a gas drill in a hut at the practice or nursery end of the ground. What wearing a gas mask, entering a gas-filled hut, then removing the mask for a few seconds was supposed to teach us I never did find out.

Friendships were quickly made and the typical evening out was usually to one of the many West End cinemas. London, of course, was swarming with people in every type of Allied uniform, and I used to think how lucky the lads were who lived in London and had their girlfriends waiting opposite the flats where we lived. It was only when they started offering prices that we realised just what service they were making available, and who they were waiting for.

Everyone was very keen and eager to get on to flying, and it was sad to see lads you had made friends with being failed in the various tests, particularly those on night vision, and sent home. However, if they survived the war, in future years they would realise how lucky they were.

After three weeks in London we received our postings and were transferred to an Initial Training Wing at Bridlington in Yorkshire, a seaside town. Our billets were the typical terraced villas on the seafront and four of us were allocated to the attic room of one of these. The only big snag was that we had to eat at the Spa complex, which was over a mile further along the seafront.

Life at Bridlington was the same routine of lectures and drilling, with the odd football match, and one game of hockey against the WAAF XI, which we lost decisively, having been overconfident and finding it hard to cope with their skill at the game and with their aggression.

The main memory of Bridlington was that we always seemed to be hungry, and we became experts in the Spa at being first in the queue for 'seconds' when they were available. There were many cafés open, but our favourite for an evening top-up of egg and chips and a cup of tea was a Salvation Army canteen, who charged about a shilling (5p). RAF pay at that stage was three shillings per day, and I allotted one shilling to my mother, which meant that I received the princely sum of twenty-eight shillings each fortnight.

The next posting was to Bridgnorth in Shropshire, which was an Elementary Air Gunnery School, and we marched happily from Bridgnorth station, up a very steep hill, to the camp. Once there we found, to our horror, we would not get out again as the camp was in quarantine, due to an epidemic of scarlet fever. After a couple of days doing nothing a party of us were detailed to go down to Bridgnorth station goods yard to help in the unloading of some equipment, and were sorely tempted when we found a baker's shop was only a short distance away. We joined the queue waiting to be served, but as luck would have it we had just been served with sticky buns, when an air commodore appeared at the door of the shop and proceeded to give us a severe dressing down. He then decided to take all our names and numbers but changed his mind when he realised the people in the queue were on our side, and finally let us go. We were quite amused to see him joining the end of the queue and hoped the baker would be sold out by the time his turn came.

Our time at Bridgnorth was cut short, and some of us were posted to the Air Gunnery School at Dalcross, just outside Inverness. We were again in a flight of thirty cadets and it seems incredible that only three survived the war. The well-anticipated moment was now drawing near and after more schooling and practice on the .303 Browning machine gun, plus cross-country runs along the shore of Moray Firth, we were allocated to Avro Anson twin-engined aircraft for a first flight. Dalcross had been equipped with Defiant fighters, which had a Boulton Paul turret behind the pilot, a similar type of turret to the one I would fly in later in the Halifax bomber, but we were the first course to use the Avro Anson.

The Anson was able to take five air gunners up at a time; the first gunner fired his 200 rounds of bullets at the target, each bullet tip having been dipped in coloured paint, which left a colour-rimmed hole in the target drogue (if he managed to hit it), then left the turret. The Bristol-type turret in the Anson was diabolical, unless you were fortunate enough to be pencil slim and about three feet tall. To climb into the turret you had to reach up at an awkward angle, grab the control handle, elevate the guns to maximum – which meant that the seat depressed – get your head and shoulders in the turret and hopefully control the seat until it elevated and fitted to your bottom.

As we were now into June of a beautiful summer, and the Anson was nicknamed the Flying Greenhouse, we were ordered to wear our battle-dress tunics, plus Mae West life jackets, as we were flying over the sea and, of course, the regulation parachute harness. By the time you actually made it into the turret you were almost drowning in perspiration. Then came the difficult bit. At the end of the first gunner's shooting, a dummy round stopped any further bullets being fired from each gun. The second gunner then had to disengage the belt from the gun, remove the dummy bullet, and insert the belt back into the machine gun, cock the gun, do the same to the second gun and he was then ready to fire his 200 rounds. The cramped position in the turret made this operation extremely difficult, and should you allow the belt to slip that was the end of the exercise. The only way to rearm the machine gun was to feed a wire down into the ammunition box and pull the belt of ammunition back up to the gun, which, of course, could only be done back on the ground.

Many were the variations from different pilots who had patiently flown backwards and forwards along the Moray Firth in company with the target towing plane, only to be told by the second gunner that he had dropped the ammunition belt, and so the exercise was aborted – the language was certainly colourful! There were the odd occasions when we were down to the last gunner and the ammunition boxes were emptied and dropped out of the aircraft door.

The course was very concentrated and became virtually eating, sleeping and flying, as with such exceptional flying weather aircraft were on the go from early morning until late evening, and leisure time was almost nil. We were always hungry, naturally, and it seemed that during that flaming June and July, the lunchtime meal constantly seemed to be something heavy like boiled fish, vegetables and potatoes followed by steam pudding or some other delight. This played havoc with many of the air gunners' digestive systems, and led to some very ill flyers indeed. I never had any trouble from air sickness at any time, so benefited greatly from the 'seconds' that were always available, especially the bread and butter pudding.

Our six-week course came quickly to an end, and in mid-July 1943 we duly attended a passing out parade and were presented with our air gunner's brevet and sergeant's stripes. Even more importantly we were given our travel warrants and two weeks' leave. Before I was posted to the Operational Training Unit (OTU) at Lossiemouth, I spent this time in Burntisland in Fife, Scotland. The town was swarming with holiday-makers, as might be expected for July, but the fair was also taking place on the Links. The war seemed far away, a perfect setting for a newly promoted sergeant air gunner to show off his uniform

On my return from leave I reported to RAF Lossiemouth and immediately started another spell of classroom work, which made me most impatient, as the one subject that seemed to give 95% of the gunners problems – aircraft recognition – I found as easy as eating my second helpings at mealtimes. It astonished me that anyone could have difficulty in recognising different types of aircraft. As it had long been a hobby of mine, I became more reconciled to the classroom grind when sweepstakes were run on aircraft recognition tests, and I picked up a few shillings in winnings.

Our billets were in Nissen-type huts in Lossiemouth itself, just off the beach. When I eventually started flying again it was most pleasant, after a night flight, to have a swim in the sea before going to bed.

The procedure at OTU was that you carried out training at your particular job, then you were allocated to a crew to continue the rest of the course together. After the air gunner's part of my course was completed, I found to my consternation that the crew I was assigned to had concluded their course and were going on leave forthwith. To compound the disaster I was informed that I had to complete sixty hours of day and night flying before my course would be considered finished, so I spent a hectic spell flying with any crew who needed a gunner in order to make up my hours.

The aircraft we were flying were Wellington twin-engined bombers, a well-tried and well-liked aircraft nicknamed the Wimpey, which carried just one gunner in the rear turret.

I was able to have a few days' leave before reporting to the conversion unit at Riccall in Yorkshire where I was due to meet the rest of the crew, and the pilot would convert from flying twin-engined aircraft to the four-engined Handley Page Halifax. I met up with some of the crew on the train from York to Riccall and we were disappointed to find there was no transport available to take us to the airfield. We were eventually offered a lift in a lorry, but had to wait until it was unloaded, the cargo being ten coffins containing the bodies of a crew and three instructors who had died when their aircraft went out of control during a fighter affiliation exercise.

The climate was a complete contrast to the summer weather we had had in Scotland, and damp horrible fog and mist was the daily ration, some days lifting to give just two to three hours' flying before closing in again. Due to the large numbers of crews being turned out from OTUs the conversion units were being overloaded and we were allocated to a new Nissen-hutted area, which had only recently been completed. Through some misunderstanding the contractor had built the usual washhouse and toilet facilities, but as they had not been part of his contract, the Air Ministry would not accept them. Having a wash and shave meant using the builders' stand-pipe, raised on two bricks to keep out of the pools of accumulating water. The situation was ridiculous but all our complaints fell on deaf ears, so we used our own remedies. We bribed the watchman with coal and coke we 'borrowed' from the RAF compound, and were then able to use the showers and toilets. A deal was struck with a local farmer for eggs, milk, etc., which saved us making the two-mile round trip to the morning breakfast, as the Mess was very overcrowded.

Our crew consisted of six in number: pilot Andy Baird from Dundee, navigator Ralph Jones from Bournemouth, bomb aimer Larry Larrabee from Canada, wireless operator Jack Horrell from Birmingham, myself as mid-upper gunner, and rear gunner Ted Wilks from Sydney, Australia. And we were now joined by our seventh member, flight engineer Gerry Mowbray from Wellington Heath in Herefordshire.

The initial flying was affectionately known as 'circuits and bumps', which was really Andy [Baird – the pilot] being converted into flying a four-engined aircraft, firstly under the eye of an instructor, then solo. We then progressed into flying the Halifax on three engines, two engines, and on one rare occasion one engine, though I must admit I was glad to see the other engines restarted. Strangely enough the next time this happened was the night we had to bail out over Germany.

The nearest town of any size to Riccall was Selby, but there was little to attract us. One occasion I remember was the Battle of Britain Remembrance Parade. Our crew was detailed to represent the station and we attended the service in Selby Cathedral on the Sunday. We were then supposed to march around Selby behind various bands and all the youth organisations, with the armed services following at the rear. The procession was a shambles, and we all walked into a pub on a corner and enjoyed a drink until our transport arrived to take us back. I recall the barman being fascinated that he had a complete crew together and giving us a drink on the house.

Our flying training progressed on to bombing, air firing, fighter affiliation and cross-country flying, which was a dress rehearsal for operational flying, giving the navigator a test and usually, weather permitting, dropping practice bombs on a bombing range. One vivid memory was a low-level bombing exercise we carried out in Bridlington Bay, where a raft was moored in the bay as a target. We came in at low level towards Bridlington, dropped our bomb at the raft, climbed to get over the cliffs, then banked round before diving back out over the sea, where we had dropped a smoke float, and Ted [Wilks – the rear gunner] and I fired our four-gun turret guns at the smoke float, all very exciting. Fighter affiliation could be another thrilling event, depending on whether the fighter played the game correctly. We took off and collected a Spitfire or Hurricane over the airfield and climbed to our operating height, usually about 18,000 feet. The rear turrets were equipped with a cine camera, and the idea was that the fighter would carry out a simulated attack, the gunner would instruct the pilot what and when to carry out evasive action, firing his cine camera instead of his guns, and in theory the bomber escaped the attack and the gunner hopefully shot down the fighter. The standard evasive action was termed a 'corkscrew'. This meant that if the pilot was instructed to corkscrew to port he would bank and dive steeply to the left, then on the way down veer over to the right, before pulling out of the dive to tilt again to the left; halfway up his climb he would bank again to the right, so that in theory he lost the fighter and ended up back on course. Very often the fighter would throttle back his speed, drop his flaps to slow further and follow our manoeuvre. It was quite alarming to see the propeller blade of the Spitfire seemingly only feet away from your turret as the Halifax was diving and climbing, particularly as the pilot would be laughing happily from the cockpit.

On one particular day we were just taxiing out for take-off on a fighter affiliation exercise when we were told to wait, and a flight engineer was brought out to our aircraft to fly with us and observe Gerry [Mowbray] our engineer at work. I was due to control the pilot from the astrodome in the engineer's position Perspex bowl in the roof, which allowed you to stand erect with your head protruding through the roof, and so view to the rear, and give Andy, the pilot, instructions as the fighter attacked. We carried out a very strenuous exercise, trying very hard to lose the fighter, and Andy threw the Halifax all over the sky. I had two rope handles to hang on to, but was forced down on my knees by gravitational forces as we pulled out of the dives. Eventually the exercise was completed, but only then did we remember our passenger the flight engineer. I have never seen anyone such a horrible colour, and he had been very ill. It also transpired that this was his first ever flight.

Chapter Seven

Ops

In mid-October 1943 we were posted to No. 51 Squadron, which was stationed at Snaith, only a short distance south from Riccall. The squadron flew Halifaxes and we were allocated to C Flight under Squadron Leader Porter. Our billet at Snaith was actually outside the airfield in the adjacent village of Pollington and our Nissen hut was located in the garden of the George and Dragon pub. Further and constant training was our lot and, of course, most of the flying was subject to the variable weather, which affected the operational flying that we were anxious to experience. One exercise involved a bomb load climb test and we were detailed to use the main runway, which crossed the main road on the airfield perimeter. The runway actually had a hump in the middle and it was only after we went over it on maximum power that we could see that one of the local buses would be crossing our path as we, hopefully, cleared the hedge. I was in the mid-upper turret looking forward and could see the faces of the passengers as our aircraft just lifted in time to clear the bus!

An exercise that was laid on in November called 'Bullseye' was to use Bomber Command aircraft to act as the enemy and test the defences around London. We were to fly down through England, out over the Channel and approach the south coast around Brighton, then fly to Slough as the turning point for our bombing runs on London, the actual target being a cross of lights in the gardens of Buckingham Palace. The weather was not good, with a lot of thunderstorms about, and we had only flown a short distance when we were coned by searchlights, which we did not lose until we cleared the south coast. Being coned is a frightening experience, and this was made worse by the weather conditions, which none of us had previously experienced. I had heard of St Elmo's Fire, but to be coned by searchlights – the pilot trying all sorts of evasive action to lose them and then to have blue flashes of electricity running around the turret from the metal parts, particularly the gun barrels – was quite alarming. We continued the exercise as far as Slough, and as we started our run towards London the call-off signal was given by the searchlights shining vertically and then dipping away from London, indicating to us that some German intruder aircraft were approaching. We then bypassed London and flew out over the North Sea and made our way north to Snaith. We were fired on by anti-aircraft guns as we recrossed the coast near Hull, but arrived back safe and sound after a six-and-a-quarter-hour flight.

We were included on the Battle Order for a raid on Frankfurt on 25/26 November 1943, and briefing was carried out in the afternoon, but doubts were raised about the weather as it was blowing a gale. Delay followed delay until eventually we took off at five minutes to midnight. The idea was that we would accompany a large force of Lancasters to a point eighteen miles north of Frankfurt, where they would turn north for Berlin and our Halifaxes would turn south and bomb Frankfurt, so confusing and hopefully splitting the German night fighters. We only found out later that the Lancaster force never took off so we were on our own.

Due to the high winds behind us the flight in was very quick. As we reached the turning point north of the target, we could see the cloud over Frankfurt, and the searchlights shining into the cloud, which made it look like a white blanket over the city. When we started our bombing run we realised there was no anti-aircraft fire to be seen, but exactly on our course the fighters had laid a double line of flares, which we had to fly between. We carried out our run and bombed on the Pathfinder markers, and were very relieved to turn away from the target area. The strength of the winds became felt as we set course into France and turned north-west to head for home. It almost seemed as if we were hovering as we struggled on our way, but eventually we left the target behind and were flying over a blacked-out France. The temperature was very low at our operating height of about 18,000 feet and we were all tiring, particularly Ted and me in the turrets trying to keep warm and alert at the same time.

Larry, the bomb aimer, was in the nose trying to pick up any rivers or points that might help Ralph, our navigator, to check our position, which he estimated to be near Paris. Suddenly anti-aircraft shells started bursting all around us. It was a very dark night, with high cloud blotting out the stars, but I could hear the shrapnel rattling about the aircraft and actually see the bursts. The starboard outer engine burst into flames and from the mid-upper I could see the tendrils of fire only some thirty feet away and shooting beyond the tail. Larry joined Andy in the cockpit and operated the fire extinguishers on the engine, and fortunately the blaze went out, but we had to close the engine down and feather the propeller. Gerry, the engineer, then cheered us up by reporting that our fuel was running low. By this time nobody was complaining about the cold or feeling sleepy, and thinking we could see a belt of searchlights ahead near Le Havre, we decided that we could not waste fuel by detouring, so on nearing the coast Andy put the nose down and we rattled through on three engines.

We were now picking up emergency calls from many aircraft with fuel shortage problems and eventually we raised Ford on the radio, which was designated an emergency field, but the best they could offer was fourteenth in line to land. Gerry was concerned about our fuel situation and also that hydraulic oil was leaking in the aircraft, which raised doubts about our flaps or undercarriage working. Finally Andy told us to take up our crash positions in the centre of the aircraft and informed the control tower we were coming straight in, which he proceeded to do successfully to the relief of everyone. We stayed at Ford for three days until the damaged engine was changed, and then made our way back to Snaith. We had not been anxious to hurry back as we were due for leave on 4 December.

Our next operation was a disaster. We took off on a raid to Leipzig on 3 December and crossed the Dutch coast without any problems. Everything seemed very quiet, and after some time Ralph came on the intercom to confess that either he had taken the wrong reading from the Gee set or the set was unserviceable. The long and the short was that we were totally lost and therefore had to turn back. We were fired at by a flak ship as we recrossed the enemy coast but, unscathed, carried on over the North Sea. We then had to jettison our bomb load, the largest being a 4,000lb cookie, and just as Larry released the bombs Ralph reminded him that there was an Allied convoy in the vicinity. Fortunately, the bombs exploded on hitting the sea and there was no action from any ships. We landed safely at Snaith very subdued and Andy and Ralph were carpeted by the CO and given a severe lecture before we were allowed to go on fourteen days' leave.

On the last night of my leave I met Bobby Russell, who had just been posted to a squadron at Pocklington in Yorkshire, also flying Halifaxes. The squadron had had heavy losses and everyone had been sent on leave until replacements of aircrew and aircraft were brought in. Bobby was not looking forward to operational flying, and I often wonder what he went through, as he had flown over twenty-five operations before being killed on a trip over France.

I arrived back at Snaith on 18 December, and we were briefed for a raid on Frankfurt on the 20th. Unfortunately, we had to turn for home due to engine trouble and we couldn't get above 14,000 feet. The starboard outer engine was changed, but on a test flight by another crew the engine throttle would not close when landing and the pilot eventually had to pull up the undercarriage to stop the aircraft. We were not sorry to lose 'C' for Charlie and were allocated a new Mark III, code letter 'H'.

Christmas was now upon us and was a very happy time, apart from briefing being announced on Christmas Day and then, luckily, cancelled.

Ralph Jones, our navigator, had been dating a WAAF from our Mess and arranged a night out for the crew at a 'quiet' country pub he had found. The seven of us met seven WAAFs in the blackout and set off to walk to the pub, all jockeying for position and trying to at least get a silhouette view of the girl who was to be our partner for the evening. Typically, when we arrived and opened the pub door the place was crammed but the landlord, realising he had fourteen potential customers, offered us his back parlour, which we accepted. One of the girls was known as the 'Jinx', as each date she had had with a crew member had been followed by the crew not returning from a trip. Ironically, she was partnered by Larry, our Canadian bomb aimer. He was unable to fly with us on 29 December, as he had been sent to hospital for some treatment.

The Sergeants' Mess Dance was a great success, although I spent most of the evening looking after Jack Horrell, our wireless operator, who became very ill. We had had a couple of half-pints of mild beer at the George and Dragon before going up to the Mess, but I think someone had spiked a drink in the Mess. None of us were 'drinkers' and especially when you knew you were possibly being listed for operations at any time and had to have all your wits about you. I missed out on the buffet but won six oranges, virtually unobtainable in wartime Britain, which we demolished the next day.

Christmas Day was celebrated with an excellent dinner, and then it was back to the training and preparation for the next operation. Foggy, frosty weather had set in over the festive season, and flying was restricted, but one day we were ordered to report to the crewroom after lunch in our PT kit for a cross-country run. Gerry Mowbray and I had made a date with two girls from Leeds for that evening, and fathomed we could not do the run and make the local bus on time. We duly set out on the run and realised the instructor had taken us over the local canal bridge and that it was some miles before we could cross back. We drifted to the rear of the field, and at the point nearest the village of Pollington we jumped and swam the canal, breaking the ice on the way, and made our way to our Nissen hut for a quick shower and change before catching the bus to Leeds. Sadly our 'dates' never turned up.

We were listed on the Battle Order for 29 December. The route was virtually straight in over Holland to a turning point north of Leipzig, then the bombing run to Berlin. We were briefed and enjoyed our bacon and egg pre-flight meal; then it was down to the crewroom to get dressed and collect parachutes. One of my duties was to collect two pigeons in containers, which each aircraft carried on the basis that should we ditch in the sea we could send off a pigeon with our position. I am afraid none of us had a lot of faith in surviving a ditching in the North Sea in winter and waiting on a pigeon making its way back to Yorkshire. Anyway I used the containers to wedge my parachute in a handy position to my mid-upper turret.

We had flying suits issued but most of us found them too bulky and restricted our movement in the aircraft, particularly if you had to move quickly. I wore the issue thermal vest and 'long johns', then my normal shirt and tie, two sleeveless pullovers, the normal issue sleeved pullover and normal trousers. I also wore standard socks, then electrically heated slippers covered by the heavy woollen seaman's stockings, which folded over your fur-lined flying boots. I then donned an electrically heated waistcoat, on top of which I wore a white polo-necked woollen sweater and finally my battledress uniform jacket. Leads from my waistcoat led to the slippers, and also to the heated gloves, covered by a pair of fine nylon gloves and then leather gloves.

As we would be flying over the North Sea we each had to wear a 'Mae West' life jacket and finally our parachute harness, with which we used a chest pack. The harness had to fit properly, particularly between the legs, but many people were careless about this, as fitted properly they were very uncomfortable to wear for a five- or six-hour flight. Many crew members left the straps, which came up between the legs, hanging loose, but in an emergency the time taken to clip them into position could be the difference between life and death. Finally we had our helmets and oxygen masks; the mask contained a microphone by which each crew member could keep in touch. With the noise of four Merlin engines, normal conversation was impossible. On night flights, we were on oxygen from take-off to landing and wearing a close-fitting mask for five to six hours was, at times, very uncomfortable, particularly for the gunners, as with very low temperatures your breath condensed and then froze. Keeping warm was a constant battle, and both gunners had the problem that, although body, hands and feet had the benefit of heated units, legs and arms did not. The turrets were very draughty, particularly as we had to keep turning them during our constant search for enemy fighters and our own aircraft. In contrast the rest of the crew were in constant argument over the heating, with the main complaint being that they were too warm.

We had the benefit of an evening take-off just before dark and everything went smoothly. The plane had maximum loading of fuel and bombs and we were soon climbing through cloud on course for the Dutch coast. With full loading, it took some time for the Halifax to reach altitude, usually about 18,000 feet, and every effort was made to get to 15,000 feet before the enemy coast as light anti-aircraft guns could reach you at that height. We had no problems until nearing the German border with Holland; an aircraft quite close to us was attacked by a fighter and returned fire. Not long after this incident the engineer reported we were losing power in our starboard outer engine, and this became sufficiently serious to close the engine down and feather the propeller to avoid drag. As we were in a stream consisting of over 700 aircraft we decided to carry on, using three engines, and in fact were able to maintain altitude until we started to lose power on the starboard inner. With this obviously serious situation we started to lose height and decided we had no choice but to turn back.

By this time we were well into Germany and could see the defence of Hanover in action on our port side, but despite jettisoning our bomb load and turning for base we could barely maintain our altitude. The port inner engine then developed the same symptoms as the others, and as our height dropped we realised we were in serious trouble. Pilot Andy Baird was having great difficulty in controlling the aircraft, with only one good engine, and it was decided we had to abandon it. Uncertain of our actual position, it was thought we might be over Holland. First to bale out was Pilot Officer Coryton; as the only officer in the crew he had taken the place of our sick bomb aimer, who was in hospital. I left my turret and collected my parachute pack, sadly leaving the pigeons to their fate.

I slipped on the chute and to my horror the pack landed on the floor, having pulled the straps, which in theory do not come undone until after the parachute opens. I folded them as best I could, holding the lot to my chest, and then had to negotiate the main spar and climb down under the cockpit instrument panel into the nose. I noticed the altimeter showed just over 2,000 feet and only the wireless operator (Jack Horrell) and the pilot (Andy Baird) were left.

I was faced with a very draughty black hole in the floor and without hesitation sat down, made sure I had the parachute handle in one hand and, holding the pack as tightly as I could, thrust myself out. I had a vague impression of the tail going past and then pulled the handle. My parachute opened with a jerk, which gave me a very stiff neck for some days, and I found myself falling gently through cloud with no idea what was waiting at ground level.

It only seemed seconds after my parachute opened that I heard the aircraft seemingly coming back towards me, but in actual fact it was going in a dive toward the ground, which it hit with a tremendous explosion. I doubted that Jack and Andy could both have escaped from the aircraft.

I started to swing at the end of my parachute and when trying to stop the movement (which I only seemed to make worse), I suddenly saw a darker area to my right and hit the ground with a thump at the edge of a field.

The cloud base had been almost to ground level and it was pouring with rain. I quickly gathered my parachute and harness together and as I tried to hide it as best I could in some bushes and shrubs the area was lit up by a vehicle on a road only a few yards away.

We had been instructed to move swiftly away from the area where an aircraft had come down, and I could see the glow from the crash site in the distance. I headed off in the opposite direction, still with the idea that I might be in Holland and could make contact with the resistance groups. I could hear music as I approached what turned out to be a village, and a dance was in full swing. It was about 7.30pm and the bomber stream was still flying overhead towards Berlin. I crept past a courting couple at a corner by walking through some gardens and made my way out of the village on the opposite side and on into the country. The rain was persistent and I looked for somewhere to shelter for the night, but any place I approached seemed to be well protected by barking dogs. I had walked for some hours when I realised that someone was following me. When I stopped walking, they stopped, and we continued in this way until I could see that I was approaching a T-junction and would have to go right or left. On my left, just short of the junction was a large tree, so I quickly moved behind it to see what my pursuer might do.

I knew immediately that something was wrong, and a torch was suddenly shone in my face and a large rifle thrust against my chest. I was aware of a man in uniform, but could not make it out apart from a small button at the front of his hat coloured, I thought, red, white and blue. I speculated that these were the colours of Holland and said to him 'Dutch?', to which he replied 'Ya.' At that point another person – the one who had been following me – approached and my 'friend' issued an obvious challenge, to which a woman's voice replied. The guard was German and obviously thought I had said 'Deutsch?', to which he correctly responded 'Ya'. He quickly searched me, and my bar of chocolate, reserved for the flight home, went quickly into his pocket and the woman disappeared, to return rapidly with a group of armed men. One, with a Luger pistol, had no doubts as to what should be done with me, but fortunately the local police chief was also present and we proceeded towards the village.

Albert was taken to a local small store where his captors managed to wake the owners.

What they were after was the telephone to report my capture, and while in the store the owner cranked the handle of his old-fashioned phone to make his call, a commotion started further down the hall. Eventually two women appeared, virtually dragging a very frightened girl about fourteen years of age, who was literally shaking. She must have had some English from school and was pressured by the adults to question me. The first quest was 'American?', then 'Canadian?', 'English?', to all of which I replied 'no'. She gave up at that and escaped back down the corridor. I must have been a frightening sight to her as my face was dirty, scratched and bleeding from landing through the bushes.

Our next stop was the local police station, where the police chief acquired a dry coat, and we were shown into the kitchen, where a large stove gave off wonderful heat. I started to steam in minutes as I was by then soaking wet. The policeman was fairly elderly, as was his wife, and sitting at the table were a middle-aged couple trying hard not to look at me. I was astounded when the door opened and a young boy of about fourteen or fifteen came into the room wearing a swastika armband and gave the Nazi salute, to which all the adults stood up and responded. The boy spoke reasonably good English and demanded to know where my comrades were and I replied they were all dead. He quickly countered by saying that was not true as they had already captured some of them, so I thanked him and it dawned on him what he had given away.

I was taken to the local telephone exchange, but now under the guard of two soldiers. I had been told to stand in the centre of the room while they occupied the only two chairs, and by then I was getting very tired as it was now around three o'clock in the morning. I edged back to a table and managed to half sit and must have been dozing when I felt a wallop and landed on the floor. One of the guards was standing over me but on the intervention of the other guard left me lying there, which suited me fine. Eventually a Volkswagen Beetle arrived and we all piled in and then had to get out again and give it a push start. Next step was Bielefeld town hall, which was a reception centre for shot-down airmen, and I immediately spotted Coryton, our bomb aimer, who called out that all the German officers spoke English. I was searched, then handed over to two Luftwaffe officers who were to escort me to the Luftwaffe aerodrome at Gütersloh, where I was placed in a cell. Later that day I was called out of the cell by two guards and escorted to the main office building. This entailed marching across the parade ground, and all the windows around the square seemed to be filled by cheering (or jeering) Luftwaffe airmen. Both guards were quite short and I stepped out to get off the parade ground as quickly as possible so I suppose it looked funny.

I was taken before a commanding officer, who was most pleasant and asked me how I felt and if there was anything I required. I requested a wash and also remarked on my stiff neck, but he was most annoyed when I said I had had nothing to eat, and my two escorts were called in and given a fair old rocket. On returning to my cell I was quickly served with a plate of soup and some black bread, which I really could not stomach, and only managed to eat some pieces of potato floating in the soup. The guards were astounded, as I had been served exactly the same food as themselves.

The next visitor was the doctor, a most objectionable little man, who roared at me to stand up, gave me a quick look over and then, still shouting, what I assumed were not complimentary remarks, walked out. It was the next day, 31 December, that I was allowed to wash and, with most of my clothes also drying out, I felt a lot better. I also found out that at least two others of the crew were in adjoining cells.

I was awakened early on New Year's Day 1944 and told I was being moved. This I found out to mean travelling by truck to Bielefeld to catch the Berlin–Frankfurt express to the interrogation camp called Dulag Luft. Six of us met up on Bielefeld station, the one missing member being Gerry Mowbray, our flight engineer. We were delighted to be reunited and eventually the guards ordered us to quieten down as some of the German civilians were getting angry at us laughing together.

We were eventually put into a compartment and the train set off on the journey to Frankfurt, which we did not reach until after dark. During the journey we all requested something to drink, but the only thing one of the guards obtained was what we called 'vichy water', much like soda water, which only made us thirstier. On arrival at Frankfurt we had to wait for a local train, a bit like a tramcar to us, and during the time I pestered the guard, who spoke some English, into getting me some water to drink. He marched me along the platform and into the station buffet, which was packed with civilians and uniformed people of all the services, and asked at the bar for water. The hostility of the barman was obvious, and you could have heard a pin drop. The guard stuck to his request and a large glass (1 litre I think) of water was placed in front of me. I played my part in drinking the lot in one go, and he calmly marched me out again.

At this point we were joined by an American airman, a little chap that we treated with great suspicion as we thought he might be a plant by the Germans to hopefully get some information out of us. It transpired that he had been on a daylight raid on Frankfurt and had been lying in the bomb bay taking photographs of the bombs going down, when a near miss from anti-aircraft fire jolted the aircraft and he fell out. He had a loaf of bread under his arm and, as we had been warned that we could be wined and dined at the Dulag Luft during interrogation sessions, we persuaded him to throw it away, which he duly did. I bet he cursed us later when he found out the 'menu' available.

On arrival at the camp, we were greeted by guards who spoke perfect English, and were instructed to remove every stitch of clothing. The temperature was well below freezing and, later, on release from the cells, I saw black frost for the first time. After our clothing was searched, we were ordered to pick up our clothes and run down a corridor, where we were allocated a cell each. The cell consisted of a wooden bunk, no blankets, a high barred window and a handle just to the left of the door, which by turning dropped a lever outside that indicated to the patrolling guard that you required the toilet. This became a lottery as everyone quickly realised that it was a way to get out of the cell for a wander in the corridor, but not so funny if you were really needing the toilet.

The first visitor was a quiet little chap who calmly produced a form with 'International Red Cross' along the top and proceeded to ask for details to fill the form up 'so that your people at home will know you are OK'. After the initial name, rank, and number he went on to squadron, type of aircraft, how you were shot down etc., which of course I refused to give him and he eventually gave up and left. His parting words were that my family would not be informed that I was alive. It all seemed a bit amateurish as a way to get information, but I found out a few days later how effective it was. This was particularly so with the American bomber crews, many of whom were shot down by fighters and suffered wounds and were refused medical attention until they 'filled in the form'. After two days in 'solitary' I was taken under guard to the office of the interrogation officer, who was very friendly. After telling me I was naughty for not completing the Red Cross form he then asked me the same questions, which I again refused to answer other than name, rank and number. The secretary, who had been taking notes, then left the room, and I realised the strong scented smell in the office actually came from the interrogation officer. Maybe he was wise, as by then I had only had a face and hands wash in five days, which I suppose was beginning to show.

He tried to draw me on which were the best defended German cities, and when he mentioned Hamburg I foolishly laughed and told him we wouldn't need to go back again as the raids in the autumn of 1943 had been very successful. He was most upset and then calmly opened a book he had on the desk, which had No. 51 Squadron written on the front, and then proceeded to tell me more about the squadron than I knew myself, even to the nickname of our flight commander, Squadron Leader Charlie Porter.

I was returned to my cell and the routine continued. In the mornings about 6am a squeaky barrow used to come along the corridor and the cell door would open and you were given two slices of black bread stuck together with a jam that was made from beetroot and a small glass of coffee that was made from acorns. I forced down the bread but could not face the coffee and sprinkled it on the floor to keep the dust down, as I tried to do some exercising to pass the time. Lunch never varied – a bowl of watery soup – and the evening meal was a repeat of breakfast.

I did not realise that the others had been released from the solitary cells until one evening a guard, with a very large vicious-looking Alsatian guard dog, took me back to my interrogation officer, who informed me I had told lies at my first cross-examination and threatened me that I could be sent down to the city to Gestapo headquarters, who had ways of extracting the truth. He probably said it to frighten me, and I tried hard not to let him see he was succeeding, but anyway next morning I was released into the hutted camp and reunited with the crew.

The following evening we were taken to the marshalling yards in Frankfurt for transportation to the prison camp. We were put into trucks that were used for moving animals, eighty of us to a truck, with straw on the floor and a bucket in the corner as the toilet. There was barely room for everyone to sit down, and a visit to the bucket meant walking over everyone, which was a difficult journey, especially when the train was on the move. We were two nights and two days in the truck, before finally arriving at the railway junction of Neuburxdorf, which was about a mile from the camp.

Chapter Eight

Captivity

It was dark as we approached Stalag IVB and the weather was very cold, with inches of snow and slush on the ground. We could see dozens of figures near the wire shouting and waving, but could not understand what they were trying to convey by their signs. We were soon to find out.

We were marched into the de-lousing area, which meant stripping completely and all the clothes were put through a chamber where they were exposed to a chemical that killed off any unwelcome visitors that we may have collected. Ordered into a room with shower heads on the ceiling we had to wash thoroughly, which was very welcome, and then into the next room where warm air blew in to dry us off. Two Italian POWs were waiting to give us a typhus vaccination, which seemed to us very crude. One scratched your arm with what looked like a pen nib, and the other daubed on some paste, but I managed to dodge that particular operation, which left many men quite ill later. The Russian hairdresser you did not miss as he sat with his cutter at the ready and we all had our hair removed, which we could not, of course, hide. The real horror caught up with me when the clothes came out of the de-lousing chamber and I, like many others, found that our flying boots were gone, taken by the Germans on behalf of their soldiers fighting on the Russian front. This was what the waving and shouting figures had been trying to warn us about as we approached the camp. The choice of footwear left to us were wooden soles with a piece of material to put your toes into, which were useless for the conditions in the camp. We were allocated to Hut 50A, which was 90% Army POWs mainly from the Mediterranean theatre, and the rest RAF.

Each hut had bunks for 200 people in three tiers, the worst being the lower bunks, which of course we, as new boys, inherited. A bunk consisted of wooden boards with a straw mattress on top and we were issued with two blankets, relics from the First World War and very thin. As the only heating came from two hotplates for cooking, which were only on a short time each day due to shortage of fuel, the hut could be very cold and draughty.

On the second or third night we were there I woke in the night feeling unwell and felt I was going to be sick. The indoor dry toilet for use after curfew was at the opposite end of the hut to where my bunk was and I realised I couldn't make it, so barefooted I took the shorter route to the washhouse, which divided us from the next hut. Unaware that there was a choked drain I found I was standing in about six inches of water that had a coating of ice, and I had broken through it, but I had no choice as I became very sick and just had to stand there. The following day I was sent on sick parade and got so cold waiting in the queue to see the doctor (Major White) that I gave up and returned to the hut. Fortunately I was never ill again until a meal was consumed when we celebrated the end of the war in Riesa on 8 May 1945.

PO Coryton had been sent to Stalag Luft III, and we were delighted when the missing member of our crew, Gerry Mowbray, turned up. Gerry had been captured quite quickly like the rest of us, but on his way to Gütersloh he made a break from his guard and escaped. Unfortunately he fell into a stream and although he managed to hide in a barn, frostbite developed in one foot and he had to give himself up to the farmer. With the problem of wooden soles and trying to walk in the slush and snow I also had trouble with frostbite, but after an issue of boots from the Red Cross I quickly recovered, as did Gerry.

Camp life was monotonous and really focused on what you might get to eat each day. We found that trying to share as a crew did not work and we split up. Andy Baird teamed up with a Spitfire pilot from Glasgow, Jack Daly and Ralph Jones, our navigator, met up with a pal and Ted Wilks, our Australian rear gunner, joined up with some Aussie pals. This left Jack Horrell, Gerry Mowbray and myself as a team, which worked very well for our time in Stalag IVB.

The camp was situated on the east bank of the Elbe near a town called

Mühlberg, which was roughly thirty-five miles east from Leipzig, and the surrounding area was totally flat. The Stalag was a transit camp for working parties going out to work for the Germans, in theory on non-military jobs. As aircrew were all sergeants or above, we could not be used in this way. We should have been sent to a Luft camp but the Germans seemed to be having trouble accommodating the numbers of aircrew being taken prisoner at that time. Being billeted with mainly Army personnel, many of whom had been POWs for some time, led to quite a lot of friction; on average, as aircrew we were much younger and the RAF discipline was much slacker. At morning roll-call we tended to mess about, always being last to fall in, and often the guards had to go into the huts to search out late sleepers, which of course led to the whole parade at times being kept outdoors for long periods.

For the first six months of 1944 we had a fairly regular supply of Red Cross food parcels, which really were life savers. Issued usually on a Monday, we were also allocated fifty cigarettes each and, as Jack was the only smoker in our group, we put twenty-five cigarettes each into a pool to buy additional food, and we each had twenty-five to spend, cigarettes being the only currency in the camp. Gerry and I usually bought a bar of chocolate, contained in the Canadian parcels, with our twenty-five, and when available a loaf of bread for fifty cigarettes came out of the pool to be shared by the three of us. The bread we tried to buy was smuggled into the camp by various people, mainly French prisoners who went out daily to work in Mühlberg. We also 'bought' from the Russians, who were employed in the never-ending job of 'pumping' the dry cesspit toilets into a large barrel-shaped container on wheels and pulling it out into the surrounding country and spraying it over the fields as manure. They were known as 'Sheissen Torpedoes' and it was easy to realise that the camp could be located in the dark by the awful odour that surrounded it, as the toilets were used by some 15,000 people. We actually went off dealing with the Russians, as we found out they were smuggling in the bread inside the Torpedo. As all deals were carried out after dark, one or two people were caught out by exchanging their cigarettes for a loaf, only to find that when they got back to the hut, the inside had been scooped out and replaced with a piece of rag, leaving only the crust.

The basic quota of food each day from the Germans was usually potatoes and either sauerkraut or a watery soup, with a portion of bread that varied at between five and ten people to a loaf. This was the basic black bread, which we understood contained a certain amount of sawdust and on eating could be believed. On rare occasions there would be a ration of margarine, and a jam that was made from beetroot, but the memorable occasions would be an issue of cheese, which could be smelled even over the 'Torpedoes'. It looked like Camembert, but even at my hungriest I couldn't face it. The most popular item was millet, usually supplied about once a month, which looked like porridge and was quite filling. Our whole lives centred around food, and particularly when to eat – either as soon as it was given out and then go to bed hungry, or wait until evening and go to bed with a full stomach. Usually the decision was controlled by when we could get access to a cooking pot and the times when the hot plates would have a fire under them, and fuel was always in short supply.

Gerry and I were fairly competent at cooking, but Jack was useless. However, we decided to give him some tuition, and as we had a Scottish Red Cross parcel that contained a tin of porridge, we set him the task of opening the tin, adding water to the contents and bringing it to the boil. This he achieved and we then supervised the sharing (equally of course) on to our eating plates, which were flattened tins with the edges turned up. Jack departed to clean the pot and pass it on to the next group, while Gerry and I tucked into our lunch. When Jack returned he stepped over the form he was to sit on at the table. As his tray must have been projecting a bit, he clipped it with his foot and it landed on his chest, and he was quite a sight with porridge running down his front and trying to rescue what he could, while accusing us of deliberately positioning the tray. We, in turn, having eaten our ration, were in near hysterics laughing at him, and to this day Jack has never been convinced that we did not set him up.

Life progressed throughout 1944 with, of course, the highlight being D-Day on 6 June and our thoughts turned to being home by Christmas. We were kept up to date with the news each evening as a radio operated in the camp for which the Germans were constantly on the hunt, fortunately without success. The search team was led by a guard we nicknamed Alpine Harry, as he always carried a climbing axe and would pick up

David Fraser

At No. 20 OTU Lossiemouth late 1940/early 1941. *David Fraser*

RAF Cranwell running up the engines of an Airspeed Oxford in 1940. *David Fraser*

David's POW identity photo. *David Fraser*

David's first crew at No. 115 Squadron in April 1941. From left to right are Geoff Hogg, Bernie Morgan, David Fraser, Alex Kerr, Alan McSweyn, and Bill Legg. *David Fraser*

Lamsdorf. *David Fraser*

David with fellow liberated POWs at RAF 122 Wing in April 1945. From left to right are Gerry Clark, Ron Chisholm, David Fraser, John Egan, and Jock Bell. *David Fraser*

Albert Gunn

Albert Gunn during training. *Albert Gunn*

Above: Albert at RAF Snaith. Left: Bomber Command air gunner Sergeant Albert Gunn. *Albert Gunn*

Albert third from right at RAF Abingdon, part of No. 38 Course, No 10 OTU. *Albert Gunn*

Albert in May 1946 outside No. 2 Mess, RAF Abingdon with friends Tony Lee and Charlie Gale. *Albert Gunn*

Left: Albert posing for a POW identity picture at Dulag Luft in January 1944. *Albert Gunn*

Charles Clarke

Charles in the back row second from right with his No. 619 Squadron crew, mid to late 1943.
Charles Clarke

Left: Scenes from the Long March.
Charles Clarke

Below: Charles Clarke's POW identity tag.
Charles Clarke

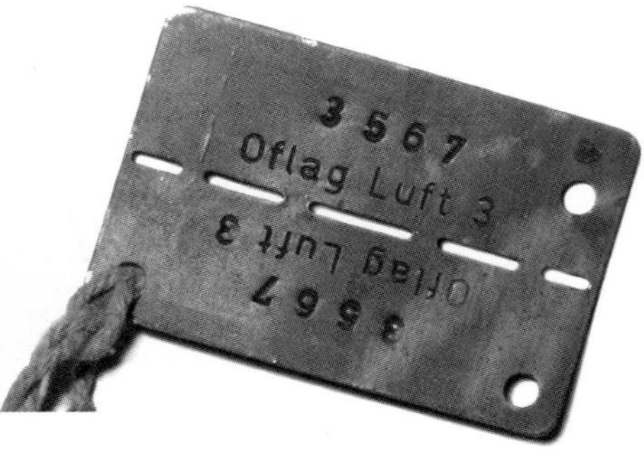

Above: Scenes from the Long March. *Charles Clarke*

Above: Scenes from the Long March.
Charles Clarke

Charles Clarke at Aden in 1967, part of the Headquarters Staff. *Charles Clarke*

Reg Barker

Bomber Command pilot Reg Barker. *Reg Barker*

The crew of No. 635 Squadron Lancaster W 'Willie' shot down on 26 August 1944. From left to right are Reg Barker, Hannes Vidal RCAF (navigator), Brian Boston (bomb aimer), 'Dick' Bird (wireless operator), 'Taffy' Kinsey (mid-upper gunner), 'Dizzy' Hemmings (rear gunner), Harry Bullock (flight engineer). *Reg Barker*

Kgf. Lg. d. Lw. I.
RJ
F/LT BARKER
5182

Name: Barker
Vorname: Reginald John
Dienstgrad: F/Lt.
Erk.-Marke: 5182
Serv.-Nr.: 124 917
Nationalität: Brite

Baracke:
Raum:

K. Liebig-Sagan

Above: Reg Barker's POW identity card. Below: Identity photos and POW identity tags. *Reg Barker*

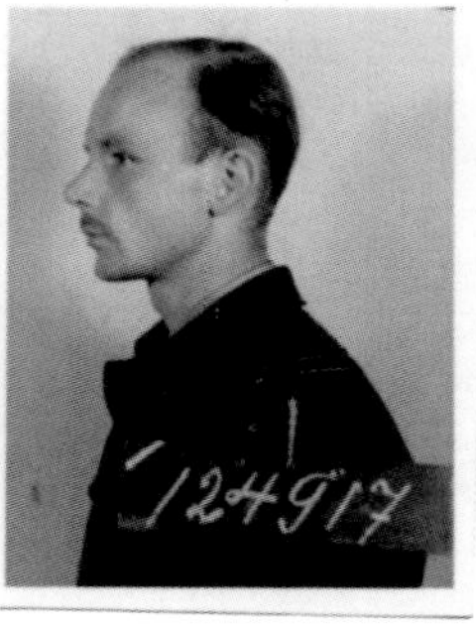

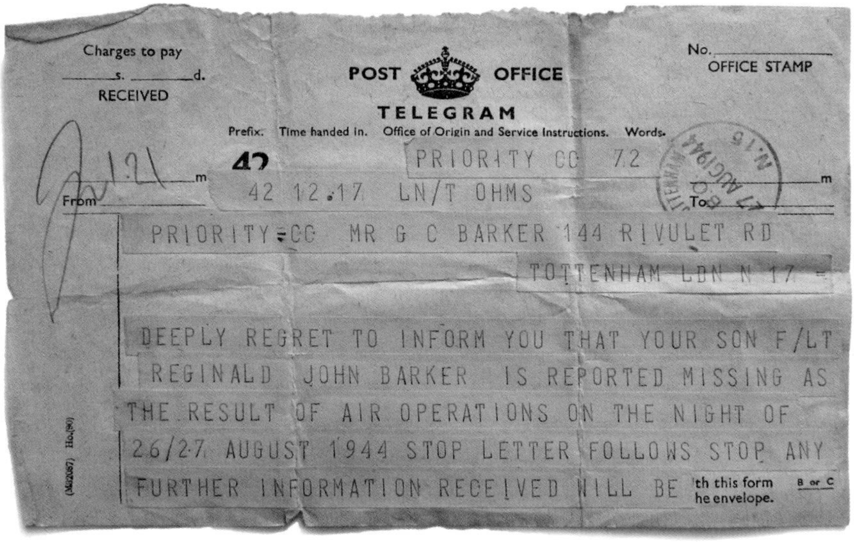

Charges to pay
_____s. _____d.
RECEIVED

POST OFFICE
TELEGRAM

No.____
OFFICE STAMP

Prefix. Time handed in. Office of Origin and Service Instructions. Words.

42 PRIORITY CC 72

42 12.17 LN/T OHMS

From____ To____

PRIORITY=CC MR G C BARKER 144 RIVULET RD
TOTTENHAM LDN N 17 =

DEEPLY REGRET TO INFORM YOU THAT YOUR SON F/LT
REGINALD JOHN BARKER IS REPORTED MISSING AS
THE RESULT OF AIR OPERATIONS ON THE NIGHT OF
26/27 AUGUST 1944 STOP LETTER FOLLOWS STOP ANY
FURTHER INFORMATION RECEIVED WILL BE

Reg's 'reported missing' telegram. *Reg Barker*

Charges to pay
_____s. _____d.
RECEIVED

POST OFFICE
TELEGRAM

No.____
OFFICE STAMP
B.O.
27 AUG 1944
N.15

Prefix. Time handed in. Office of Origin and Service Instructions. Words.

42

From____ To____

IMMEDIATELY COMMUNICATED TO YOU STOP PENDING
RECEIPT OF WRITTEN NOTIFICATION FROM AIR MINITRY
NO INFORMATION SHOULD BE GIVEN TO THE PRESS = OC
DONWHAMMARKET +

CT 144 N 17 26/27 1944 LN/T +

For free repetition of doubtful words telephone "TELEGRAMS ENQUIRY" or call, with this form at office of delivery. Other enquiries should be accompanied by this form, and, if possible, the envelope. B or C

Henry Wagner

Henry in the early days of his Royal Air Force career. *Henry Wagner*

Henry, seated third from the left at No. 5 Air Navigators Course. *Henry Wagner*

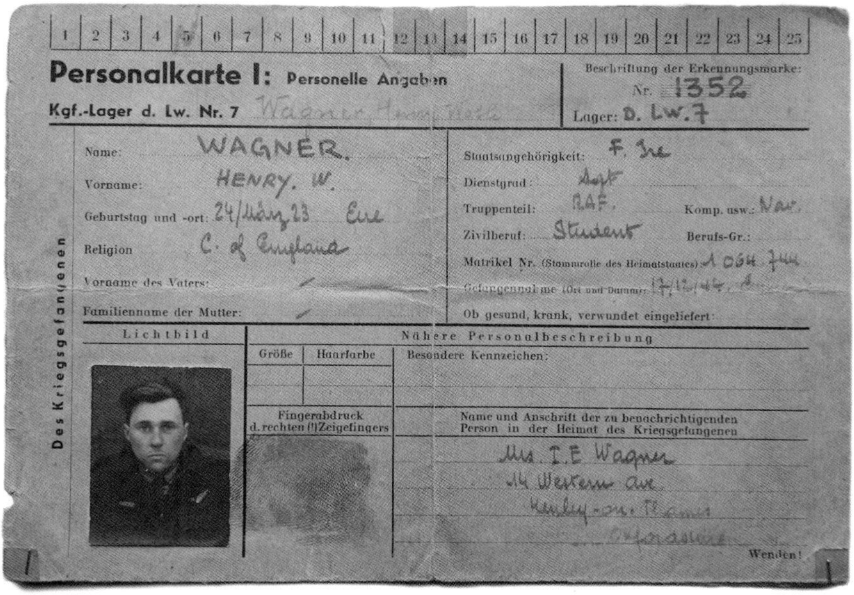

1 | 2 | 3 | 4 | 5 | 6 | 7 | 8 | 9 | 10 | 11 | 12 | 13 | 14 | 15 | 16 | 17 | 18 | 19 | 20 | 21 | 22 | 23 | 24 | 25

Personalkarte I: Personelle Angaben

Kgf.-Lager d. Lw. Nr. 7 Wagner Henry Will

Beschriftung der Erkennungsmarke: Nr. 1352

Lager: D. LW. 7

Des Kriegsgefangenen

Name: WAGNER.

Vorname: HENRY. W.

Geburtstag und -ort: 24/März 23 Eire

Religion: C. of England

Vorname des Vaters: —

Familienname der Mutter: —

Staatsangehörigkeit: F. Ire

Dienstgrad: Sgt

Truppenteil: RAF. Komp. usw.: Nav.

Zivilberuf: Student Berufs-Gr.:

Matrikel Nr. (Stammrolle des Heimatstaates): 1 064 744

Gefangennahme (Ort und Datum): 17/12/44.

Ob gesund, krank, verwundet eingeliefert:

Lichtbild

Nähere Personalbeschreibung

Größe | Haarfarbe | Besondere Kennzeichen:

Fingerabdruck d. rechten (!) Zeigefingers

Name und Anschrift der zu benachrichtigenden Person in der Heimat des Kriegsgefangenen

Mrs. I. E. Wagner

14 Western Ave.

Henley-on-Thames

Oxfordshire

Wenden!

Henry's POW identity card. *Henry Wagner*

Americans operating their cooking stove known as 'blowers'. *Henry Wagner*

Feeding quarters for a 'combine' of six. *Henry Wagner*

Luckenwalde, bringing up the barrack block's daily ration of soup. *Henry Wagner*

Liberation at Luckenwalde. *Henry Wagner*

Russian liberators at Luckenwalde. *Henry Wagner*

Sleeping arrangements. *Henry Wagner*

Henry visiting the resting place of his crew at Venray War Cemetery. *Henry Wagner*

some unfortunate's bunk and tear it apart in his futile pursuit. He was unaware that the moment the team appeared in the camp it was shadowed until its departure.

During the summer of 1944 an event took place that caused us an upheaval. A New Zealander named Ward had escaped from a camp in Italy when that country dropped out of the war in 1943, and he had joined a partisan group fighting in the mountains. He was eventually captured by the Germans, who considered him a criminal, and he had been charged with murder. He was due to stand trial at the civil court in Dresden, which was only about twenty miles from our camp. The bulk of the RAF prisoners were in a small compound of eight huts, and on the morning Ward was due to go to Dresden he was taken to the de-lousing chamber to be freshened up for his journey. The route from the punishment cells to the showers meant crossing the camp main road and as he returned with his guard, dozens of RAF prisoners surrounded him and eventually when the main guard were called out and restored order, Ward had disappeared. Shortly after this event all the RAF personnel in the Army huts were ordered to transfer to the RAF compound, which annoyed me slightly as I had managed to get a middle bunk by this time. However, the reason for this move became only too clear a few days later.

By this time I found out that another Burntisland lad, Andrew Smith, was in the RAF compound, having been shot down in the Bay of Naples, and we made contact. I also became friendly with a chap called Peter Barrington, who was in the peculiar situation of having an English mother married to a Luftwaffe officer. Towards the end of the war Peter's mother was smuggled into the camp, under great secrecy, and sheltered until our liberation. Her story was told in a book published after the war by Jack Stoneley entitled *Jenny's War* and made into a television series.

As a newcomer I inherited the inevitable bottom bunk and found to my astonishment that beneath my bunk, and all the others in the hut, were dozens of the briquettes that were issued for supplying the hot plate stoves for cooking. The RAF had 'acquired' a key to the coal store and during the dark nights raids were carefully planned and carried out to ensure heating for the coming winter.

One morning, roll-call was instigated as usual, with the normal casual response, until on leaving our building we found each hut surrounded by SS troops with machine guns set up and covering the whole compound. The black uniforms and aggressive attitude made us recognise that this was a serious situation, and we were instructed to parade with all our belongings ready to move. We realised quickly that when we were taken to Dulag Luft we all had our photographs taken and given a POW number – mine was 269775. We had to go before a group of Gestapo sitting at a table, who checked us off against our photographs. We were then told to make our way to the far end of the camp near the main entrance and move into the huts being vacated by the Dutch POWs. All the Germans' efforts were in vain, though, as Ward was not discovered and in fact lived the rest of our time in captivity within the camp.

One plus from the move was that we were checked out early and I acquired a top bunk in our new hut (No. 14A), the first on the left after entering the camp. We were a complement of 200, virtually all RAF, except for one or two Army people. The Germans treated Royal Artillery soldiers as RAF, as in the German forces the anti-aircraft equipment was operated by Luftwaffe personnel, and through this we made friends with two Royal Artillery sergeants – Cyril Wright from Hull and Len Jackson from Fordingbridge in Hampshire. Sadly Cyril was to lose his life in 1948 while on duty trying to keep the Jews and Arabs apart in Haifa.

After being under the Army discipline of a regimental sergeant major we now had a change, as the man elected was a corporal in the Parachute Regiment, who had the respect of everyone and made an excellent hut commander. A big minus from our move was that we lost all our coal stocks to the Dutch.

Life continued into the autumn of 1944, when it became painfully obvious that we were not going to be home for Christmas, and we realised another winter lay ahead in the camp. I had received my first letters from home in May, and therefore was relieved to know that everyone at home knew I was alive. A red letter day was my twentieth birthday, when 28 letters arrived for the 200 in the hut and I received 22 of them – to say I was unpopular would be an understatement! We had reserved a packet of custard to celebrate my birthday, but on cooking it discovered it was full of flour weevils, but Gerry and I concluded that they must be cooked, so with Jack refusing his share we demolished the lot.

An escape tunnel had been started from the library hut, which was nearest the perimeter, and constant appeals for bed boards to use in shoring had made some of the beds a bit uncomfortable. Sadly, when the tunnel was virtually completed, a tractor working on the fields of potatoes growing outside the camp fell into the exit tunnel and gave the game away.

One method of escaping was for an RAF sergeant to swap identities with, say, an Army private going out on a work party, as it was reckoned much easier to escape from a farm where you had been sent to labour. Many of the French worked locally and went out daily to Mühlberg. They were loosely guarded, but the French, of course, lived under the threat that, prior to the invasion, the Germans could take reprisals against their families.

As autumn came so the delivery of Red Cross parcels became less regular and we entered a most difficult time. We were cheered by the noise of the RAF bombers at night, and could watch in daytime the wonderful sight of the American air force flying overhead, although seeing many shot down, one crew landing by parachute literally at the gate of the camp.

Christmas was not a happy event, and we had by then organised our parcel issues into all tea and coffee being placed in a communal pool. This meant that by using the boiler in the washhouse adjoining the hut less fuel was used, and the tea and coffee lasted much longer, which was a benefit to all.

During December the Germans carried out an offensive in the Ardennes area, which had a significant effect on our lives. Large numbers of soldiers from the American 106th Division were captured; all these men had only been in the Army a few months and had been placed in this particular area to allow some more experienced troops to have a rest, on the basis that the Germans could not or would not do anything aggressive until the spring. We were informed that 100 Americans would be allocated to each hut and room was made for them. We solved the problem by knocking out the centre board between two bunks and sleeping three in the space provided. Once again I had to move and so lost my top bunk, as I joined Jack and Gerry in the middle tier, but at least it was warmer. The addition of an extra 100 men in an already overcrowded hut led to a lot of friction, but eventually things settled down.

Living conditions deteriorated due to the bad winter weather, with poor food rations and the decline in delivery of Red Cross food parcels, but at least we were uplifted by the thought that we would, hopefully, see the end of the war once the weather improved.

Delivery of mail from home was also affected and we kept looking for parcels, as the three of us had all requested cigarettes to be sent when we wrote letters home. As mentioned before, cigarettes were the 'currency' used in the camp. In early April I was informed that a parcel had arrived for me and I duly reported, with my colleagues, to collect it. To our great disappointment, the German guard opened the package to reveal two Penguin paperbacks, one on birdwatching, the other title I forget, but our hopes were certainly dashed. Two days later I was again told there was a parcel waiting for me and this time we all felt we must be lucky. Lo and behold I received, from the same Aunt Bell who had sent the paperbacks, a diary 'Frae Bonnie Scotland', which I still have as a souvenir.

The first entry in the diary was made on 9 April 1945 recording the arrival of twelve Red Cross trucks from Switzerland with 6,500 Canadian and American food parcels; also medical supplies. The following day we were issued with one Canadian and one American parcel between three people, which were very gratefully received.

The weather had improved greatly by then and was lovely and warm. On the evening of 13 April we saw American Thunderbolts at low level for the first time. Excitement was rising within the camp, and speculation as to who would reach us first, Allies or Russians, made up most of the conversation in the camp. Thunderbolts carried out strafing nearby on 14 April. On the 15th American Mustangs were over by 9 o'clock in the morning and again in the evening, and in between American Lightnings had a go at a train stopped in Neuburxdorf only a mile from us. Rations being issued were declining badly: turnips, potatoes and bread – 75gm.

On 16 April, Mustangs, Thunderbolts and Lightnings were over throughout the day and anything that moved, either on the nearby River Elbe, or by rail or road, was attacked. On 17 April aircraft were over at 07.15 hours and I was duty cook for our group. Lighting our fire under the hot plate had been delayed as a Russian POW had been repointing part of the brick chimney. I was lying on our bunk reading when we heard an aircraft flying very low and suddenly open fire. I wasted no time in dropping to the floor and was very quickly followed by some others who had been awaiting the chance to cook. We heard a second aircraft in a dive and then the very frightening sound of machine guns firing. I was at the bottom of the pile of bodies between the bunks and could feel something wet soaking into my clothes. Eventually, when we thought the aircraft had gone, we all started to move, and fortunately were all unhurt and the wetness had been caused by someone knocking over the Russian worker's bucket of water. Some of our tier of bunks had been hit, including our particular two, but fortunately without any casualties. The cause of the incident had been a working party of POWs who had been taken out of the camp to a nearby wood to collect firewood, and had stopped outside the camp for a rest and roll-call before entering again. The pilots of the two American Mustangs responsible had assumed they were German soldiers and attacked, but unfortunately (or deliberately) continued their firing into the camp itself. Five POWs were killed and eight injured and of course everyone was shaken by the experience.

On 19 April we witnessed a heavy bombing raid by American B-17 Flying Fortresses on an airfield only a few miles away. I also saw a Messerschmitt 262 (the twin-engined fighter used by the Luftwaffe) shot down by a Thunderbolt as it tried to make its way back to the airfield, obviously damaged. In the evening Thunderbolts attacked a fuel and ammunition train only half a mile away and every truck was destroyed. Air activity stopped by 21 April and we could hear artillery and small-arms fire around, and we woke on Monday 23 April, the Germans having left, to the sight of a lone horseman from the Red Army riding into camp, then turning around and riding off again, after giving instruction to the Russian POWs.

I had my first trip outside the camp on the following day, and was appalled at the amount of looting and destruction carried out to a house we visited. Cyril and I walked to Mühlberg on the Wednesday and were astounded to find the town looted by hundreds of POWs. We were issued with hardly any rations and Cyril and I returned to camp with a box of tinned milk in small cans. The camp was without lights and water and we were able to trade for more suitable food to keep our group going. I had my first egg since 29 December 1943 on Thursday 26 April 1945.

Despite our hopes of getting home quickly, and countless rumours, nothing happened. On 1 May the Russians put up some decorations to celebrate May Day, and proceeded to have a party in the old guard block. Many of us took the opportunity to raid the office block and remove all our records which, in the case of RAF men, included photographs. The Russians were most upset and insisted that we all fill in new forms, giving personal details. I often wonder what some poor Russian clerk made of it all, as nobody gave their real name or address in the UK as requested, but it became a competition as to who could think up the daftest answers. Days went by, with food again the prime concern, and to go far from the camp scrounging was becoming a dangerous game. The Americans were moved out on 2 May but by the 4th our rations were raw potatoes and still no lights or water in the camp.

Russian guards were put on duty in the camp by 5 May and then on Sunday the 6th we left Stalag IVB at last at 2.30 in the afternoon. We crossed to the west bank of the Elbe at Strehla and arrived in Riesa about 7.30 in the evening, very tired but glad to be on the move. We were astonished to be welcomed by the Germans with cold drinks and invitations into their homes, and our group of five peeled off into the home of a lady with a mentally handicapped daughter. The reason for the invitation became only too apparent when we saw how the Russian army of occupation conducted itself. Any woman of any age was fair game for the soldiers and the women had found that having an Allied serviceman in their house meant that a Russian could not enter.

A force of Russians with green bands on their caps moved into the town and quickly asserted their authority over everyone, and all the Allied POWs were rounded up and billeted in an ex-German panzer unit barracks, unfortunately without any beds, so we had to sleep on the floor. Food was still scarce and we set off to forage for provisions. Gerry (our flight engineer) and I found some allotments where we acquired some vegetables and Gerry used his country upbringing skills by acquiring a rabbit from a hutch in one of the gardens. Dehydrated potatoes were found by some of the others and Jack (our wireless operator) located a cider factory to which Cyril and I returned and obtained a jar of cider. The factory had two very large tanks, where we assumed the cider was allowed to ferment, and when we arrived two Russian soldiers were seated by the outlet valves trying to get cider to drink. The large valves were hopeless to try and fill a glass as the cider frothed badly when the valve was opened. One of the soldiers got impatient and riddled both tanks with his sub-machine gun and we watched while cider poured out of the tanks up to their knees and they happily scooped it up to drink, at which point we decided it was time to leave. The date was 8 May and we listened to Churchill giving his famous speech before settling down to our celebration dinner.

To say the dinner was unforgettable would be an understatement, as I have never been so sick in my life and various reasons were given. The rabbit was not cooked enough, the dehydrated potatoes were 'off' and the cider was too raw. Whatever the reason, I have not knowingly eaten rabbit again. To make things worse the Russians, who had now put a guard on our billets, celebrated VE Day by firing off a large quantity of captured ammunition that was lying all over the place. They seemed to take great pleasure in firing at the barracks window, which in our miserable state meant getting to the toilet was difficult.

The days passed, with rumour following rumour that we were to be moved. The weather was excellent but finally on 23 May we were ordered to parade at 12 midday and then marched out of the town at 2pm. A fleet of American Army lorries turned up about 4pm, and eventually we were loaded aboard about 5pm and arrived at a base on the airfield at Halle, near Leipzig, about 7.30 in the evening, soaking wet from the rain, but very happy. We were taken straight into the Mess hall, where plates were laid out with a most odd meal we thought. A piece of corned beef, some peanut butter and a piece of 'white cake'. We had been building ourselves up on the journey for steak and chips etc., but none of us could finish what was on the plate, it was too rich. The white cake was in fact white bread. We were really well looked after by the Americans and on Friday 25 May 100 Dakotas arrived on the airfield and we left at 2pm for Brussels, where despite having an engine failure we reached safely. We were taken to a hostel and given about £10 in Belgian money and all of us went into the city. Travel on street cars was free, I remember, but have no recollection of what we did, although I think we had a meal. I do recall arriving back at the hostel in the early hours of Saturday 26 May very tired, and gazing at the lovely white sheets on my bed. The door opened and the lady in charge of the hostel announced that we had to get up for breakfast immediately (4.30am) and then travel out to an airfield. We were a bedraggled lot when we arrived to find that the weather in England was bad, and it was early afternoon before Lancasters started to appear and we were allocated to one of them.

I tried to get into the mid-upper turret as a Lancaster is not designed for thirty passengers, but another chap beat me to it so I had to rough it in the fuselage. The weather was pretty awful over the Channel and I had no sympathy for the mid-upper passenger as he was very sick.

We landed at Oakley and boarded a train at Oxford for Cosford, near Wolverhampton. Our carriage had been reserved and we got a little satisfaction from seeing a group of Army officers ordered out to make room for us. Our reception at Cosford was tremendous and, having got rid of every stitch of clothing we had brought back from Germany, we were kitted out completely with new apparel before falling into bed. Sunday morning we completed medicals etc., and by lunchtime had been issued with travel warrants and transport to take us to Wolverhampton. Transport during wartime was very unreliable, and only one train was due to travel to Scotland that day. Typically it was on time and we missed it by a few minutes. We were advised to catch a train to Leeds, but again missed the connection and eventually ended up in York, where a long wait lay ahead for the night train from King's Cross to Edinburgh. Eventually the train chuntered in and, of course, it was standing room only, but a group of us found some space to sit on the corridor floor in the carriage adjacent to the tender, which stored water for the steam engine. We all got settled and the train got under way and was soon rattling through the night at speed. We were all dozing off when suddenly the dividing door next to the tender burst open and we were drenched with water. The reason was that engines picked up water while travelling and something had gone wrong, hence we got an early bath. I eventually arrived in Edinburgh Waverley about 5am, a wet, miserable morning, and had to waste time until I caught the first train to Burntisland where I arrived about 6.40am.

As I walked up to my mother's at 26 Rossend Crescent, I met one of her neighbours heading off to work and her greeting was: 'They are not expecting you.' Despite the many replies I might have given her, I said politely: 'I'm sorry about that but I'm not going back.'

Mother's door furniture was shining bright from its early morning clean, and I went to the back door and into the kitchen. My mother was cleaning out the living room fireplace and on looking up said: 'I thought it would be you.' I had assumed that she would have known I was on my way, but the telegram I sent off from Cosford on arrival on the Saturday was delivered to my Mother later that day, Monday 28 May. At least I was home, very tired and weighing just under seven stones against the eleven and a half stones I had been in December 1943. After my father and brother, George, had gone off to work in the local shipyard, I went to bed, but had little chance of getting any sleep as the door bell was constantly ringing as neighbours called.

The local pipe band turned out in the evening and a dance was held out in the street. I was presented by two of the neighbours with a handsome sum of money, which had been collected to welcome me home.

I was on leave until 11 October when I was ordered to report to Church Fenton in Yorkshire, which was being used to deal with returned POWs. The idea was that we should have some time to make our mind up what we wanted to do – either leave the RAF, continue as before, or remuster to some other trade. I elected to stay in the RAF and put down a return to flying as my first choice. I still hoped to get a pilot's training, a forlorn hope really as now the war in Europe had ended, the RAF had a surplus of pilots. My second choice was as an airfield controller and I was posted to a Transport Command unit at Desborough in Northamptonshire to carry out airfield controller duties until sent on a course at Broadwell near Swindon. Typical of a military organisation I completed the airfield controller's course in February 1946 and was then posted to No. 10 Operational Training Unit to join a crew and resume flying. Abingdon was a very pleasant pre-war airfield with excellent facilities. I was allocated a room in the NCO's Mess, which I shared with one other chap, Tony Lee, an ex-POW like myself. We were quickly crewed up and I joined a crew with another ex-POW named Warrant Officer Pepper, who soon after gained his commission and became a pilot officer and was known by us all as Pep. Pep had been a pre-war boy entrant to the RAF and was shot down in France in 1940, flying Fairey Battles, and spent nearly five years as a POW. Now he had to learn to fly Wellingtons.

The rest of our crew were all 'new boys', but we quickly formed a very good unit and became the best in the course at crash drills, dinghy escape drill etc. I suppose Pep and I were still very conscious of the importance of escape drill and getting out of the aircraft quickly. Some of the instructors could not work out why we carried out so many dinghy drills on the river near Oxford. We did enjoy the river outings, but our main reason was that we had discovered a lovely riverside café, which made beautiful pancakes as you waited and served them dripping in hot syrup – a much better way to spend time rather than listening to some lecture or other.

The eight months I was at Abingdon were very pleasant, and I spent a lot of time training, exercising and regaining both weight and fitness. I had taken up squash, and started to play cricket with the help of our other air gunner in the crew, Jimmy Dunbobben. Jimmy was from Lancashire and a very good cricketer, and we were both selected for the station team, Jimmy for his batting and me for fielding as I certainly could not bat or bowl very well.

Football was another favourite sport and I was introduced to serious running when we were ordered to the sports field one afternoon. All aircrew seemed to resent being forced into anything, and when we were told that we had to enter for three events, nearly everyone volunteered for long jump, high jump and the 100-yard sprint, on the basis that you would be eliminated quickly with the least effort. A pal I had made, called Don Thomsett, and I were a little late arriving that afternoon and found we had to run in the mile race. Also, being unaware of the craftiness being shown by so many, we tried our best and were the first and second to finish. This meant we were selected to run for the aircrew against the rest of the station, and were then nominated to represent the station at the Training Command sports day. We took our training very seriously and I suppose it did us no harm, but on the day trailed in a long way behind the winner, who had actually represented Great Britain the week before.

At the end of September 1946 we left Abingdon for a conversion unit at North Luffenham in Rutlandshire to start flying the four-engined Lancaster. We were there only three weeks when the whole unit moved on 24 October to Lindholme, an airfield outside Doncaster in Yorkshire. Pep quickly converted from the twin-engined Wellington to flying the four-engined Lancaster and we now had the addition of a flight engineer to our crew. Our engineer was a squadron leader who, as he was Irish, was never addressed as anything other than Paddy. Pep had found it difficult to adjust on Wellingtons to flying very rigid speed, height and course and many were the arguments between pilot and navigator. Paddy extended the arguments by standing alongside Pep on take-offs and landings and anticipating his instructions. I noticed quite often from my seat in the rear turret how low we were on take-off when Paddy would retract the undercarriage before Pep had given the order. It led to a lot of banter from the rest of the crew.

Training proceeded well until 18 November when we carried out a bombing exercise. The weather had deteriorated so badly we were diverted to Finningley, only about five miles from Lindholme, but had the benefit of three runways against our two, and made landing easier in the gale force wind that had developed. We retired happily to the Mess for tea, but were then informed that the aircraft was required back at Lindholme for night flying. As Pep had not converted to flying a Lancaster at night an instructor was to be sent over to fly us back.

All our gear was thrown in a heap through the rear entrance door, as we only had a take-off, join circuit and land to do, and I took my position in the rear turret. As we came in to land the wind was obviously strong, with heavy showers of rain. The instructor talked Pep down and we landed with the usual three-point bump but rose slightly and the wind immediately drifted us off the runway on to the grass. The grass was long and very wet and the brakes had no effect, and so on we went with all of us wondering what lay beyond the end of the runway that might stop us. Fortunately there was a dip in the ground, which threw the aircraft on to its nose and we came to a halt. Unfortunately I was about thirty feet in the air with my turret doors open, but the tail suddenly dropped and I was able to get out and join the rest of the crew. Pep walked up to the ground level and held out his handkerchief, which whipped out horizontally in the wind. At the inquiry into the accident the weather man gave evidence that the wind was 5mph and calming and no one else was allowed to give evidence, so poor Pep got an endorsement in his logbook, which we all thought was very unfair. To complete our night the Elsan toilet fixed at the rear of the aircraft tipped over in the accident and deposited its contents over our clothes and equipment.

It was eight days before we flew again and settled down to our course. Flying was consistently affected by the poor maintenance on the aircraft, and in early January 1947 I was given the choice of being demobbed or signing on as a regular in the RAF.

I decided to come out and left for the demob centre near Blackpool. The country was in the grip of the worst winter snow for many years and I had a horrendous journey by rail from Doncaster via Sheffield across country to Preston. We were quickly equipped with our civilian clothes and I left the RAF on 10 February 1947 to return to my old job at the Naval Air Yard, Donibristle.

1	2	3	4	5	6	6	7	8	9	10	11	12	13	14	15

Name:

Charles Clarke

Bomber Command Bomb Aimer
Failed to Return from a 24/25 February 1944 Raid to Schweinfurt

Chapter Nine

The Volunteer

I was born so long ago I have forgotten. Actually it was 25 November 1923. I grew up in various places in London and then, in 1941, I joined the Royal Air Force. I was told to report to Deansbrook Territorial Barracks, where I had my first medical. I had been told as a child that I had a weak heart so I wanted to show I was fit. There was another man there who wanted to prove how unfit he was.

Charles was sent to Oxford, staying in one of the colleges, where he underwent medical examinations, his education was scrutinsed and he appeared before a selection board. 'Overnight we were put into a cinema in the high street and it was full of camp beds about six inches apart. The camp bed next to me was occupied by a sergeant air gunner who was operating on Whitleys. I was horrified about the losses and I began to wonder if I was doing the right thing, joining the air force.'

I went before the Board, chaired by a squadron leader, and eventually I was sworn in and given a number that stuck with me until I was commissioned. They then gave me a little lapel badge of the Royal Air Force Volunteer Reserve. During the war, there was no permanent position; everybody was a member of the volunteer reserve. A couple of weeks later I was told to report to Swiss Cottage near Regent's Park Zoo. I was there for about a week where we were examined again and were vaccinated against various diseases. We went to a garage near there where we had our kit thrown at us. I was in a flat in Hall Road with about sixty-odd bedrooms, just filled with boots, great coats, kit bags and everything. We used to dine in what is still the café at the zoo. We were under training aircrew. A chap with me was a LAC and he was almost like God. I had about three haircuts in a couple of days to satisfy his lordship the corporal. I might just as well have shaved it at the beginning.

I was posted from there to Scarborough, one of many Initial Training Wings that had been set up at seaside and holiday resorts, where hotels were taken over. I was in the main hall of Scarborough College. The stage was just behind my bed. We were taught hygiene, law, administration, navigation, signals. We had to do Morse code, ten words a minute, and master signalling with Aldis lamps.

I thought we were then going to be sent overseas for training but went instead to Heaton Park. Initially we were in a Nissen hut with one big boiler that no one had seen before and a big coke stove in the middle. Then, for a matter of weeks, I was accommodated in a private house, four of us in a small bedroom. Gosh, it was a rough area of Manchester. You'd hear folk come out of the pub at the end of the night and a chap beating his wife. You were learning about reality. From there I was posted to Carlisle, where we flew Tiger Moths.

Unfortunately I caught mumps and I was taken to hospital in Longtown, Wales. I think I was the only patient with seven or eight nurses. I was there for a few weeks and when I got back I had been dumped – taken off the course and posted back to Heaton Park. I honestly cried. I was so set on me becoming a pilot. Looking back, however, I realise that if I had become a pilot I would probably be dead by now – the majority of pilots were killed because they were the last person to get out of the aircraft.

They tried to put me in a Nissen hut but by then I had been elevated to a leading aircraftman with a propeller emblem on my arm. I used to walk along almost looking at my illuminated arm, I was so proud. I said I wanted to be lodged in a private villa, and after a lot of argument I managed to persuade those in charge. They took me to a house where a young lady, who couldn't have been more than about twenty-two, claimed that she couldn't accept me. I was with a billeting officer and with reluctance she had to admit me. Once I was there I could understand her reluctance to take in a young man like myself because she had only been married a few weeks and her husband was on night work.

Charles, no longer destined to be a pilot, now began training as an observer: 'The four-engined aircraft had come in by then and they were desperate for crews so there was no option.' He was posted to a flying school at Dumfries, to continue training on Bothas and Ansons. 'The Botha was a flying coffin – a short operational career. It was so underpowered. To my surprise I was commissioned. I was given a chit enabling me to go to Burberrys and get a uniform and I became a pilot officer.' Charles's next posting was to an Operational Training Unit, to become part of a crew acting as a bomb aimer.

We were flying on Wellingtons. There was a wonderful method of crewing up – so scientific. It was really like a dating agency. You were all put into a room or a hall or a hangar and then you sorted yourselves out, 'I like the look of you' etc. I crewed up with a Canadian pilot and an older navigator. They were both older than me but the navigator was a very old man, he was twenty-six. From here we graduated to the Heavy Conversion Unit at Swinderby, on to Lancasters, and here we picked up the rest of our crew, including an Australian gunner. Next we were posted to Woodhall Spa. The Officers' Mess was the Petwood Hotel – the best Officer's Mess in the country.

Charles and his crew now embarked upon operational duties with No. 619 Squadron, entering the air battle at one of the most intense periods of the Second World War.

We were there during the Berlin offensive, over November and December 1943 and January 1944. It was certainly not the time to be in Bomber Command – the losses were great – very high. After the war I went to Poznan cemetery and I saw a grave with three people there – unusual because the graves were so close together. I looked at the register and to my surprise they were on my squadron. There was only one squadron in the Officers' Mess and you knew everyone, but I didn't know them. So they could have been on their first or second trip or when I was on leave. We lost about three COs in about six months. It didn't matter how good your crew was, it was a matter of whether you survived. If there was an enemy fighter in your area and he beamed on to you, you'd had it because, for a start, he had a higher-calibre weapon, probably a .5 cannon, whereas we had a .303. He had probably come from a warm bed and our rear gunners had been in a rear turret for about five hours. He could home in on you because they were homing in on our tail warning radar 'visual monica'. He had upward-firing guns so he could lay off and fire. Our gunners never saw him so it was just a matter of luck whether you survived.

When I was in a prisoner of war camp the guards would close the hatches on the huts when there was a bombing raid so we never saw aircraft, American or British. When we were on the march much later, going towards Lübeck, we saw several raids and it was pathetic to witness aircraft being hit; some exploded immediately, some caught fire and crashed. You'd count the parachutes coming out and you'd think, poor so and sos – you knew how many were in an aircraft. It was sheer luck whether you survived. The losses were fairly heavy. One of my friends was shot down in January and I went to see his parents who were Salvation Army officers in Tunbridge Wells. I said keep your fingers crossed as he may be a prisoner of war. After the war I found out he was actually killed. I kept in touch with the parents and his brother who became director of music in the Salvation Army, and one time, at Christmas, I got a letter from his sister, enclosing a letter he had sent from Woodhall Spa speaking about his girlfriend and saying he went to a 'Kinema in the Woods with Charles Clarke'. I said to my daughter at the time that it was written by someone very immature, but you were all bloody well immature then.

The No. 619 Squadron diary records the arrival, from No. 1660 Conversion Unit,of Charles and his crew on 15 August 1943: Pilot Officer E.K. Williams (pilot), Sergeant J.R. Trail (flight engineer), Pilot Officer A.G. Knight (navigator), Sergeant P.B. Smith (wireless operator), Flight Sergeant J. Glazebrook (mid-upper gunner) and Sergeant William Walch (rear gunner). Erle Williams was soon in action, acting as a 'second dickey' on Flight Lieutenant Jones's crew for the raid to the German V-Weapon research station at Peenemünde on 17/18 August 1943.

On 30 August Erle Williams took his crew on a raid to München-

Gladbach. On return the crew reported on what they had seen and the experiences they had had, Charles in particular describing the actual bombing of the target. The squadron diary records: 'The primary target ... was attacked and bombed from 19,500 feet at 02.45 hours. Weather conditions: clear. The target was identified by red and green T.I.s bombs [Target Indicators] being dropped on single red T.I. in bomb-sight. Fires appeared to be burning well around both aiming points. Nickels [leaflets] were dropped. Red T.I.s appeared to be rather scattered, red and greens being in separate clusters; bombing on southern target rather scattered. Some defect in W/T on journey home, and aircraft filled with smoke so that we thought we were on fire; this caused us to get off track and cross coast at Dunkirk. Fault traced to transmitter which was switched off and smoke cleared. Photo showed small town with railway track partially obscured by smoke.'

On 2 September the crew carried out 'Gardening' (mine-laying) in an area described as 'Nectarine 1' and reported on their return that 'Vegetables [mines] were placed on Gee fix at 21.46 hours from 6,000 feet.' What follows is a summary of Charles's raids, with short extracts from their post-raid reports giving a, somewhat understated, impression of the sights Charles would be witnessing from the nose of his Lancaster.

5 September, Mannheim. *'The target was identified by red and green T.I.s. Numerous fires fairly well concentrated.'*
3 October, Kassel. *'Large concentration of fires seen in centre of target. Glow from fires seen 120 miles away in return journey.'*
7 October, Stuttgart. *'Weather conditions 9/10th cloud. Only the glow of fires was seen. Nickels were dropped. 15/20 'Cookies' seen to be jettisoned in the Channel on outward trip.'*
18 October, Hanover. 'Weather conditions *9/10th cloud. Red T.I.s appeared to be very scattered; bombing also scattered.'*
26 November, Berlin. *'The target was identified by ground and sky markers, bombs being dropped on green T.I.s. Large fires seen burning: a large explosion seen in target area at 21.57 hours. A satisfactory raid and bombing concentrated.'*

2 December, Berlin. *'Bombed from 20,400 feet at 20.21 hours. The target was identified by cluster of three green T.I.s and two wanganui [sky marker] flares, centre of green T.I.s being bombed. A large red fire seen in target area. Numerous markers scattered around position "X" over a 40/50 mile area.'*
3 December, Leipzig. *'Weather conditions 9/10th cloud. The target was identified by a cluster of wanganui flares and one green T.I. on the ground, bombs being dropped in cluster of flares.'*
16 December, Berlin. *'The target was identified by wanganui flares, and green and red T.I.s, bombs being dropped on furthest cluster of green T.I.s.'*
20 December, Frankfurt. *'Very large explosion seen at 19.48 hours. Glow of fires visible 120/140 miles away.'*

Around Christmas 1943 Charles's crew was briefed for a raid and on arrival at their aircraft's dispersal they found their Lancaster completely iced up. 'I was standing on the wings sweeping the ice off. Even on the ground it would have been dicey. As it was the op was cancelled.'

29 December, Berlin. *'Weather conditions 10/10ths cloud, tops at 12,000 feet. The target was identified by PFF [Path Finder Force] markers; bombed MPI of three wanganui flares. Glow of fires seen for 150 miles.'*
5 January, Stettin. *'Smoke covered target area. Bombing accurate at first but more scattered later. Red glow and smoke seen from Sweden.'*
27 January, Berlin. *'The target was identified by PFF markers; bombed MPI of four wanganui flares. Nothing seen except small glow of fires in centre of flares, though fires seemed to be developing well.'*
30 January, Berlin. *'Wanganui flares seen whilst run up very concentrated, but later scattered. Scattered areas of fires seen after leaving target.'*
19 February, Leipzig. *'Weather conditions 10/10ths cloud … PFF marking was good, and target seemed to be well alight judging from reflection on cloud; no estimate of effectiveness can be given due to cloud. Rear turret reported prior to take-off as defective given OK by duty corporal armourer, was still defective – guns could not be depressed.'*

20 February, Stuttgart. *'Concentration of T.I.s very good. No large fires seen, though thought fires were starting in the town. Forecast winds again too strong – had to orbit 15 minutes.'*
24 February, Schweinfurt. *'Nothing was heard from this aircraft subsequent to take-off.'*

On 24 February 1944 Charles and his crew set off just after 8pm from Coningsby to be part of a 734-aircraft attack on Schweinfurt. At the end of the night 33 crews had not returned to their UK bases, including that of Charles Clarke.

We were hit, the aircraft was on fire, the wing was blazing and there was no doubt which way we were going. I got up and pulled open the hatch and waited for the first person to get behind me. I didn't fancy jumping out only for the rest of them to get back. I got out and counted because I was afraid my chute might be caught in the aircraft. It was all dark. I had had training in parachuting – I had jumped off a six-foot ladder on to a bale of straw once and that was the only instruction I ever had.

Charles, along with three of his crew, would survive the incident. His pilot, Flying Officer Erle Williams, RCAF, and gunners 25-year-old James Glazebrook, RAAF, and 29-year-old William Walch, lost their lives and now rest in Durnbach War Cemetery in the south of Germany. Charles, having escaped the burning aircraft and successfully deployed his parachute, was now floating down into hostile territory.

I came down in the snow and got my map out, in the dark, and started walking towards what I thought was Switzerland. I kept falling into the snowdrifts and disappearing. I could see myself being found in the spring just preserved, if you like. I was exhausted and what's more I saw footprints of animals around and I was terrified because I thought they were wolves.

Eventually I had to hide up and found a hut. I was so tired and cold. I thought I would try and light a fire because it was a very remote area, so I got my escape matches out and they were bloody useless. They kept breaking – just tiny toy matches. I had decided to cut some slithers of wood off and start a fire because there was a kind of stove. The knife broke. So much for an escape kit.

I started ploughing on and eventually I had to come down on to the road. There was no way you could go across country. I thought I was doing well until I went round a bend and there were some Germans. Afterwards I found they had put a cordon round for an American crew that had come down. I was alongside a river. It was iced over and I wondered whether I could run across it. I was just about to try when they fired a shot. For me the war was over. What was interesting was they just couldn't believe how young I was. I looked young but they thought the British were flying schoolkids. I was taken to a gaol – I didn't know whether it was police or Gestapo – and put in a cell. I started shouting to find out if anyone else was there. The Germans, impolitely, told me to shut up so I thought what else could I do? I started singing the song 'Missed the Saturday Dance … Don't Get Around Much Anymore'. It was so appropriate. To my surprise I got someone else singing it, but to this day I don't know who it was.

Eventually I was escorted by the Luftwaffe to an airfield. We were in the guardroom, a Feldwebel and two airmen, and one of them had a Sten gun, which he fired and it went just over my head. I honestly thought he had tried to murder me but the Feldwebel tore him off a strip. I was then taken to Frankfurt am Main and Dulag Luft, the interrogation centre. We had little cells that were heated – after the war some guards were prosecuted for overheating the cells – and were asbestos lined. We were interrogated, the usual thing of giving name, rank and number. It was incredible, as they told me more about the squadron than I knew. I was there for about a week – very, very hungry and had to shout if I wanted to go to the loo.

Finally, I was taken by some guards to Frankfurt station, and the people there wanted to lynch me and were spitting. After all, we were Terrorfliegers. I was pleased we had the guards to protect us. We boarded the train and occupants in the compartments were told to get out and make room for us. I finished up at Sagan. Recent arrivals were described as milk bottles – as we were operating at night we didn't see the sun. The climate was Continental extreme cold and extreme heat. In the summer we wandered around with just a loin cloth and we oversunned ourselves. We had no knowledge at the time of the after effects of exposure to the sun.

Once in the camp I was questioned by our own people. They were looking for stool pigeons. Then I was taken to a room of sixteen, and I had a top bunk.

Chapter Ten

No Longer a Sport

At the National Archives, Kew, the series WO 344 holds questionnaires filled out by liberated prisoners of war. Charles's is included but only contains very brief factual information. Two of his former crew members' questionnaires also exist. That belonging to ex-POW James Trail reported that after Dulag Luft he had spent time at Stalag Luft VI in Heydekrug and Stalag 357 at Thorn and then Fallingbostel. He had also tried to make an escape, 'from marching column near Luneburg, April 15'. Peter Smith's ex-POW questionnaire also reported time at Stalag Luft VI, Heydekrug, Stalag 357 at Thorn and finally Fallingbostel. He recorded suffering two months of acute gastroenteritis owing to bad sanitation, and when asked if he had received adequate medical treatment, he replied: 'Yes, under the circumstances.' In regard as to whether he had been interrogated: 'Yes. Dulag Luft. ... Prolonged solitary confinement in small overheated room with little or no food. Threatened handing over to Gestapo when refused to give information but suffered no beating up.' The questionnaire closed with the question: 'Have you any other matter of any kind you wish to bring to notice?' Peter was keen to mention the impact a certain 'Dixie' Deans had had as conditions were worsening in Germany. 'Wish to bring to the notice of the British Government the fine work of W/O J.A.G. Deans, Camp Leader of Stalag Luft 6 and Br. Man of Confidence at Stalag 357. It was due solely to his untiring efforts that so many improvements in conditions at the above mentioned camps were effected.' Speak to any ex-POW and everyone who came across Dixie Deans holds him in the highest regard for the way he motivated his fellow Kriegies in the last desperate months of the war, and tirelessly sought to keep them out of harm's way.

Charles Clarke arrived at Stalag Luft III virtually two years after the camp opened. Situated in a pine forest just outside the town of Sagan in Silesia the camp had been constructed to accommodate the growing numbers of Allied airmen falling into enemy hands. As the war progressed, and the air war escalated, the camp expanded, with new compounds being opened. Charles found himself housed in North Compound and was in time to witness one of the most daring and audacious prison breakouts of the entire war. Subsequently immortalised under the title 'The Great Escape', the initial aspiration was to see 200 men break free. Charles, having recently arrived in StalagLuft III, had not been party to all the preparations. 'We knew it was going to take place because people who had been selected to go through the tunnel – mainly older ones with language skills – had moved into a hut near the tunnel.'

On the night of 24/25 March 1944, having crawled through tunnel 'Harry', seventy-six men managed to escape into the woods beyond the wire, before the entrance to 'Harry' was discovered. As Charles recalls: 'During the night we heard a shot and we knew the game was up and they had been discovered.' Only three of the escapees would go on to make home runs, and twenty-three would be returned to captivity. Which left 'The Fifty' who, under the direct orders of Adolf Hitler, were murdered.

The morning after the Great Escape we were paraded and held out in the bitter cold, we really had very little clothing. They counted and recounted, with no help from us, trying to establish how many people had absconded. This went on for several days. The senior Allied officer was a chap called Group Captain Massey, who had a gammy leg. He was repatriated soon after the Great Escape and was able to give first-hand information to Parliament, following which Anthony Eden stated that these murdered men must be revenged. The Germans also issued us with a warning.

NOTICE
To All Prisoners of War
The Escape from Prison Camps in no Longer a Sport!

Germany has always kept to the Hague Convention and only punished recaptured prisoners of war with minor disciplinary punishment.
Germany will maintain these principles by International Law.
But England has besides fighting at the front in an honest manner instituted an illegal warfare in non combat zones in the form of gangster commandos, terror bandits and sabotage troops even up to the frontiers in Germany.
They say in a captured secret and confidential English military pamphlet.

THE HANDBOOK OF MODERN IRREGULAR WARFARE:
'The days when we could practice the rules of sportsmanship are over. For the time being, every soldier must be a potential gangster and must be prepared to adopt their methods whenever necessary.'
'The sphere of operations should always include the enemy's own country, any occupied territory, and in certain circumstances, such neutral countries as he is using as a source of supply.'

England has with these instructions opened up a non military form of gangster war!
Germany is determined to safeguard her homeland, and especially her war industry and provisional centres for the fighting fronts. Therefore it has become necessary to create strictly forbidden zones, called death zones, in which all unauthorized trespassers will be immediately shot on sight.
Escaping prisoners of war, entering such death zones, will certainly lose their lives. They are therefore on constant danger of being mistaken for enemy agents or sabotage groups.

URGENT WARNING IS GIVEN AGAINST MAKING FUTURE ESCAPES!
IN PLAIN ENGLISH:

Stay in the camp where you will be safe!
Breaking out of it is now a damned dangerous act.
THE CHANCES OF PRESERVING YOUR LIFE ARE ALMOST NIL!
All police and military guards have been given the most strict orders to shoot on sight all suspected persons.
ESCAPING FROM PRISON CAMPS HAS CEASED TO BE A SPORT!

One major problem in the POW camp was the uncertainty, particularly after the murder of the fifty. What would happen to us? We had no idea what they were up to. There were conjectures – would they do this, would they do that. We all thought that after the invasion we would be out very quickly. It never occurred to us that it was going to take nearly another year. We had the BBC News and the Germans broadcast their news. We kept a map going based on their bulletins rather than ours. There is a story that the commandant asked our senior officers, 'Where exactly are they according to your news?'

We were very short of food. We had one small stove in the room which threw out a little heat and occasionally you might be able to do a brew on it, but not very much else. There was a kitchen in each hut, which served about 100 people, and you were allocated a twenty- or thirty-minute slot during the day, so the cook had to prepare everything and make sure he got it on that stove. When I talk about cooking I mean making something out of corned beef, or making a kind of tart out of ground biscuits. You got a biscuit on the table and using the top of a cocoa tin, which probably had flies on it, you would rub it on the table and grind it down.

The loo – the abort – was a distance from the hut and all it consisted of was a big rail with rows of holes and a big pit. Very smelly, you were all sitting side by side chatting and there was a term known as an 'abort rumour'.

They closed the shutters at dusk and the lights went out at 10 o'clock. There was a time called the quiet period in the afternoon; you were not allowed even to whisper because everyone was reading. It was a deliberate attempt to enjoy some peace and it was self-imposed, it wasn't the Germans insisting.

We were very short of food, and often we didn't receive a Red Cross box. Occasionally we would get a German loaf of bread made out of sawdust and you could almost see the splinters in it. In the whole camp there was one bread-making machine and sometimes you could book a slot on that – but rarely. You would cut the loaf as thinly as you could so that you could get as many slices as possible. They would be brought back and the slices put on the table. Then you would cut cards for the choice of slice just in case one had a splinter more than the other. Occasionally Kriegie 'glop' – God knows what it was – had weevils floating in it. It came in a pail and you ladled it out and cut cards for who had the choice of bowl and then you would cut cards again to see who would lick the container out.

The currency in the camp was cigarettes. Each food parcel had fifty in them but, of course, the Americans' and Canadians' were duty free and for some reason or other the Germans allowed those in. We had an exchange shop called Foodacco and everything was priced in numbers of cigarettes. A chocolate or Hershey bar would be a thousand cigarettes. I used to save my cigarettes and get a Hershey bar. I would clean my teeth at night – we had no toothpaste – and then I would get into my pit, as we called it, get a little knob of chocolate, put it in the middle of my tongue and see how long it lasted. It was quite a treat.

There were lectures on all manner of subjects. I remember going to one on psychology. We would go to church on Sunday, and usually shave and put on a tie. At least I had a better wash on a Sunday.

A few ice-skates were allowed. On the sports field we built a ridge and filled the inside with water, bucket by bucket – labour was cheap – and turned it into an ice rink. There was ice hockey between the Canadians and the Americans. The most popular sport, because it required very little equipment, was volleyball, which I had never seen before. The high spot was the cricket match between Australia and England – a mini test.

None of the Americans were involved in the Great Escape. The Germans had opened up another compound and transferred all the Americans into it. It was wondered how they would ever get the information about the British news. It would take them a long time to acquire the bits for a wireless set. Someone hit upon the idea of shouting the news from our compound to their compound. Now that was quite insecure. When the news was read we had our own guards all round to make sure there were no goons in the vicinity, but the trick was to shout it across in Gaelic and their padre spoke Gaelic, and one of our chaps, and the chances of the Germans knowing Gaelic ...

With the greater air activity there were more POWs and Americans did start coming in again – two or three Americans in my room. One got a card from Wyoming inviting him to become a sheriff, which we thought funny, him being all of twenty-three. One of the Canadians was the toughest, roughest person I have ever met. He had been in the American Marines, then when the war broke out he crossed the border and joined the Canadian Air Force. He had been in hospital three times with VD and before that he had fought in boxing booths in cinemas. Some of his sayings were revolting. He was a rough chap and the last I heard of him, he had settled back in Canada and had a stars and stripes at the end of his garden. He had a wife and three kids and I often wonder if his wife knew his background.

Towards the end of January 1945 Russian troops began to close in on Sagan. At a meeting at Adolf Hitler's headquarters on 27 January, there was a suggestion that the Stalag Luft III POWs be given the choice of staying put or being evacuated, which would require transport. Hitler intervened. 'Imprisoned officers could not receive better treatment than our own people ... our traffic situation did not permit the transport of even our own people by means of railway trains or in large columns, and the population had to tramp along the roads even in winter.' Hitler insisted the inmates would 'have to go even if they trek on foot'.[3] Various destinations ... were allotted to the 12,000 POWs of Stalag Luft III, which included the transfer of men from North Compound, including Charles, westward to a camp called Marlag und Milag Nord.

When the Russians came near, and they were twenty miles away, you could hear the guns, and we were delighted that we were going to be freed. Suddenly, the Germans decided to move us. We probably had an inkling of this a day or two beforehand because I had made a pack – I'd got a shirt and stitched it so I could put it on my shoulder, and in the last hour or so I had made a sledge. We were marched out in the early hours of the morning [28 January] and it was minus 28°C, there was a blizzard, and we weren't dressed for it. The Germans had made no arrangements for food or accommodation and we didn't even know where we were going. Anyway we marched – trudged rather than marched actually – and it was thirty-six hours before we stopped, outside a barn. There were camp beds but the people who didn't get in got frostbite and the chaps who took their boots off had trouble getting them back on because the footwear was frozen.

The following day we tramped out. The guards didn't really know what was happening. It became slushy underfoot at one stage and we had to abandon the sledge. I was in what we called a combine – three of us: myself and two others both from No. 617 Squadron. On one night, however, it was delightful – we stayed in a glass factory and it was warm! I remember holding a little tin, a Yorkshire pudding, and putting that in a glass oven, cooking it and then munching it.

Eventually we reached Spremberg, and the warehouses by the station. We were put in cattle trucks, about fifty in each, and I had no idea where we were going. We all had dysentery by then and had just one bucket for each truck.The advantage was it was en suite, but you can imagine the stench.

Charles's train arrived at Tarmstedt station, to the north-east of Bremen, on the afternoon of 4 February 1945. The POWs then, in the rain, had to drag themselves a few kilometres more to what had previously been a camp for captured Navy personnel, Royal and Merchant, called Marlag und Milag Nord. Despite being tired and rain-drenched a six-hour wait followed before they could enter their new confines. Their mood did not improve when they did finally enter the camp.

It had been wrecked completely. The stoves had been broken, all the windows had been smashed, the beds had been burned, and there was just straw on the floor. It had been a prison for the Navy and they thought they were being evacuated to make way for refugees from Hamburg and Bremen. Food was running short and I spent the whole of one morning on my haunches collecting, in a little tin, small bits of coke from a cinder path that we could burn and get a brew. One time, a bread wagon was approaching the camp and was attacked by one of our own aircraft and shot up. If that pilot had come down we would have lynched him.

On 10 April, with the British Army advancing, Charles and his colleagues were on the move again, their German captors leading them in the direction of Lübeck.

By this time the weather had improved slightly and we lived permanently in the open. Then we crossed the Elbe, and when we got to the other side there was a Dutch barge called the SS *Capella*. I went to try and scrounge something and they offered to shelter me. Really it was as a hostage, so I said no, because the first thing the 21st Army Group was going to do was bombard the opposing side of the Elbe.

As if there was not enough for Charles and his colleagues to deal with, there was also the danger of being mistaken as enemy troops by Allied pilots going for targets of opportunity. 'We used to put out our towels to show 'POWS' and that was the time when we saw our own aircraft being shot down.' As they neared Lübeck the senior British officer, Group Captain L.E. Wray, inspected their allotted camp, finding it totally unsuitable. Charles recalled his visit.

There was typhus, so there was a lot of argy bargy and we were put into a farm, once again without any shelter, by a lake just outside Lübeck. Then a little scout car came into the camp, an officer and an NCO, and we surrounded it. He wasn't the advance guard, I think he had lost his way, as he was well ahead of the main body who eventually came and told us to stay in the camp. They said they would provide transport to take us to Brussels, where there would be a reception and we would be flown home. I decided that wasn't for me. With two No. 617 Squadron chaps from my combine, I borrowed a car that I had no intention of returning. We ran out of fuel and then hitchhiked. Two majors said they would take us halfway to Brussels, which they did, and they gave us a piece of paper to show at the senior Officer's Mess, headquarters, 21st Army Group rear, saying: 'These are three friends of mine, look after them.' We hitched again, with two women, got to Brussels and went to the 21st Army Group rear headquarters. We showed them the paper and they said: 'You can't stay here.' I thought what a bloody nerve. They said, 'Get in the car', and we drove through Brussels, pulling up by a hotel. I thought: 'Well, this is a bit better, they are really trying.'

One of the POWs who accompanied Charles during his time in captivity and on the march was Jim Cooper. Jim had flown pre-war as a radio navigator with Imperial Airways on their 'C' Class flying boats. Retraining as a pilot Jim eventually found himself flying with No. 617 Squadron and was shot down on 24/25 April 1944. During their march Charles recalls: 'It was Jim and his navigator who were with me. I later heard that John had been killed in Malta and when I visited the island I searched in the cemetery and I couldn't find anything.' A number of years after the war Charles tried to find out what happened to them, discovering that they were both dead by then, Jim Cooper having been killed in an aircraft accident in Malta in August 1946. Flying in a BOAC Dakota as a radio officer, Jim lost his life when the aircraft, having developed engine and fuel problems, returned to Luqa, crash-landed and burst into flames. Jim was unable to escape from the aircraft having been trapped by an engine, which was part of the cargo, that had come loose.[4] In recent years Jim Cooper's son managed to make contact with Charles and went to visit him. 'He was born after his father was killed; I didn't know he was married. I look back and I think why didn't I contact them at the time. But when you come back, and communication wasn't as good as it is today, you were so busy with your own careers, and getting married. In my case I very soon went overseas. Anyway I invited the son and his wife here. He said "For the first time in my life I think I know my father."'

Returning to 1945, Charles would take his place as one of the thousands of ex-POWs repatriated to the UK as part of Operation Exodus.

I borrowed ten quid off an NCO, which was a lot of money then – to buy myself a pair of shoes and after a few days in Brussels we thought we really ought to get back. We eventually flew back in a Lancaster, were sent to London, and put in some seedy boarding house, telling us we must stay there and not leave. Well, we were through the window and hitting the high spots straight away. The following morning we were taken to Cosford and were billeted in the Fulton block. Then the grateful government, for whom we had suffered, gave us some coupons for a pint of milk a day for six weeks. Great stuff.

After the war Charles remained in the Royal Air Force, achieving the rank of air commodore, and was also awarded the OBE. Since retiring Charles has been instrumental in preserving the memory of his former Kriegie and Bomber Command colleagues as President of the Royal Air Forces ex-Prisoners of War Association and Chairman of the Bomber Command Association. Approaching his mid-90s Charles remains extremely active, frequently attending and speaking at functions, supporting the Air Training Corps, and regularly making the trip to Stalag Luft III in Sagan for commemorations of the Great Escape and the Long March.

Indeed, he has recently been invited to go to Germany to the place where his Lancaster came to ground in February 1944, and to visit a memorial dedicated to the three airmen who were killed in the incident. In light of this Charles has set about trying to find anyone related to Erle Williams, James Glazebrook and William Walch, and if any reader has any information the publisher of this book would be pleased to hear from them.

1	2	3	4	5	6	6	7	8	9	10	11	12	13	14	15

Name:

Reg Barker

Bomber Command Pilot
Failed to Return from a 26/27 August 1944 Raid to Kiel

Chapter Eleven

Obviously the RAF

Reg Barker was born on 11 December 1921 in Luton, Bedfordshire, but grew up in Wood Green, London. His father, John, had been an engineer in the First World War and subsequently went to work for Vauxhall Motors, but when the company got into financial trouble John lost his job. 'He had to go back to Wood Green, where he had been brought up, where his mother lived, and some of his siblings.'

I left school in 1938 at the age of sixteen and a half and went into an insurance company in London. When war was declared I was at home on my own on that Sunday morning and I heard Chamberlain's speech on the radio. I stepped outside the house and lots of neighbours were out in the street chatting and wondering what it was all going to be about. Suddenly, the air-raid warning sounded about half an hour after Chamberlain stopped speaking, which seemed rather alarming. It proved to be a false alarm – whether they did it on purpose or not I have never known.

When the bombing did start my father – my mother Bridget had died in October 1939 – insisted that we went out into the shelters in the garden. This became rather boring after a time and we decided to sleep in our beds. One night I heard a bomb coming down and I rolled under the bed. The bomb exploded about half a mile away. I heard the explosion and that was the nearest I came to actually being bombed. We were at the cinema when the house next door was bombed, and while it was very seriously damaged, our house was relatively unscathed.

We were evacuated to Totteridge, to a country house near to the sights and sounds of Hendon aerodrome. We used to see the Hurricanes taking off – rather exciting. You could see the vapour trails. You listened to the radio of course and we heard the stirring speeches from Churchill – he was amazing.

On my nineteenth birthday in December 1940 I went to a recruiting office in Edgware, to sign up for the Royal Air Force. Obviously, it had to be the RAF, having come through the Battle of Britain and the bombing of London, and the RAF was the in thing wasn't it. The Army had been defeated, they had lost all their tanks and vehicles in France. It would take a few years to build it up again. There wasn't actually a victorious Army but there was a victorious RAF. You don't have to think about motivation when your country is under attack. The Germans wanted to invade us and they very nearly did.

I was inclined to think I would rather like to be a fighter pilot. That was the glamorous job that was being publicised at that time, the Brylcreem boys. When I was being interviewed, I was asked about my past life. The Boy Scouts was a big feature in my early days. I joined the Cubs when I was six, then became a Scout and a patrol leader – a King's Scout actually. We were very patriotic in those days. I still am. I wondered afterwards whether the reason they decided I would go into Bomber Command rather than Fighter Command was because I had been responsible for six young boys. Whatever job was offered to me it seemed enjoyable. I was only nineteen when I started flying in the United States. In fact, I went solo a day before my twentieth birthday – very young, very privileged and very exciting too.

Having signed up for the Royal Air Force, Reg then had to wait. 'I was eventually called in to go to Uxbridge to have all the medical tests and so forth and I was accepted for air crew.'

I went to Regent's Park Air Crew Reception Centre and spent a couple of weeks marching round and eating in the zoo cafeteria, with a corporal shouting out, 'Come on you goons, come on you goons', chasing us along. They provided us with what they called irons, which was a knife, fork and spoon and you had to dip them into a big tub of cold water and swill it around – that was the washing up.

Reg was soon posted to Torquay in Devon, to start his RAF training, and recalled marching up and down the seafront 'in the glorious summer of 1941'.

That was in the morning. In the afternoon, we used to go up the hill to Babbacombe to learn serious navigation, flight navigation, meteorology, etc. We found it very difficult to stay awake after having PT all morning in the hot sunshine. But we managed. Then we were sent up to Liverpool and shipped over to Canada. We were slung in hammocks, I think it had been a banana cargo boat, a solid mass of humanity who seemed to swing, but it was the ship that rolled and we only felt we were swinging. As we approached Canada we saw the exciting view of the coast with the red maple trees contrasting with the green conifers.

We landed at Halifax, Nova Scotia, and went by train to Toronto. On arrival there the most amazing thing happened. The Canadian Air Force kitted us all out in grey flannel suits and black berets. We had to put our uniforms in our kit bags. Then we continued by train down and across the great lakes, travelling beyond Detroit and all the way down to Alabama and Georgia. Initially we stopped at Montgomery, Alabama, and spent a couple of weeks doing rifle drill with the American Army.

Reg's flying logbook records that he arrived at the US Air Corps Primary Training School, Darr Aero Tech, Albany, Georgia, on 10 November 1941, departing on 14 January 1942. While there, and a few days before Reg's twentieth birthday, 'the Japs bombed Pearl Harbor. President Roosevelt described December 7 as a day which will live in infamy.'

All the instructors spoke like cowboys. We had been brought up on black and white films, of course. Cowboys were pre-war and it was a great experience. The initial training was on the Stearman. It was a thrill, absolutely. The very first time I looked over the side, I thought 'crikey', it was an extraordinary adventure. On this very first flight there was I, sitting in the aircraft with the instructor, and the horizon was moving all the time, the horizon was moving. We were sitting still and the horizon was moving. An astonishing feeling. After a very short time you discover that actually it isn't really like that at all, the horizon is still there, but you are not. But that was the uncanny sensation I remember having.

On 19 January 1942 Reg arrived at the US Air Corps Basic Training School, Gunter Field, Montgomery, Alabama, departing in March and arriving at the US Air Corps Advanced Flying School, Craig Field, Selma, on the 19th of the month. 'The second part of the training had been on the BT 13, a monoplane with fixed undercarriage, and after completing that course I went to Selma where we were flying the wonderful Harvard, a beautiful aeroplane with retractable undercarriage and fixed wings.' Following the earlier attack on Pearl Harbor, Reg recalls: 'Suddenly, the Americans became very active. They wanted to expand their air force, and were laying concrete aprons so they could bring in more aircraft and extended the training programme. They then needed instructors to help build up their air force so that is why I was retained an as instructor.' Reg had arrived at Napier Field, Dothan, on 3 June 1942, remaining there until 26 March 1943, with the occasional detachment to the Single Engine Gunnery School at Elgin Field, Florida.

There were American pupils and RAF cadets. In the case of the American pupils, I was just twenty and they were twenty-five and twenty-six. They must have wondered what they were doing being taught by a schoolboy. That is why I grew my moustache to make myself look a little bit older. When they announced that they wanted volunteers to step forward and become instructors none of us had wanted to – apart from one chap who was intending to marry an American girl. I didn't want to volunteer. We were going to miss the war and that was what we were in it for. It would all be over before we got back to England.

Initially it was a disappointment, but we soon settled in and enjoyed it every much. The wonderful thing was that being at an American station, we as instructors could fly at any time – take any aircraft that was available. My favourite shift was to fly from 7.30 in the morning to 12.30, with one pupil every hour; 50 minutes' flying and ten minutes' landing and so forth. Having completed five hours with five cadets I would finish at half-past twelve and then go back and have lunch – not having taken any breaks of course during that morning session. I would have a shower and I could then take up any Harvard that was available and any visiting aircraft that did turn up – a P40 Tomahawk on one occasion. We were near the Gulf of Mexico and we could have the most terrific winds and storms come in. One time I was flying a little Auster and I had to land across the runway, actually across the width of the runway because that was the way the wind was blowing. The ground crew were waiting to grab the wings as I landed.

I had graduated and got my silver American wings on 16 May 1942. I can never forget that date, it was the proudest day of my life.

Eventually Reg was posted back to England, looking forward to seeing his family and the next stage of his RAF career. In May 1943 he left Canada on the *Empress of Scotland* and on his return to the UK he was sent to Harrogate and then No. 14 (P) Advanced Flying Unit, Banff, arriving on 15 June 1943.

I was converting to twin-engined aircraft and had a wonderful time flying all around Scotland on my own – up the hills and the mountains. It was fantastic – just about over the top and down the other side. Didn't have to pay a penny for it either. Petrol was free and it beat any other experience.

Over the next two and a half months, flying from Banff and also Fraserburgh, Reg accumulated flying hours on the Airspeed Oxford.

I must have had the feeling that it was all taking a long time. There was always the problem that there were probably never enough aircraft for the pilots who were trained, so it was a long lag. I arrived back in the UK in May 1943 and I wasn't on operations until May 1944 – nearly a year later, for no other reason than, evidently, Bomber Command could not absorb us or didn't have the aircraft for us. Anyway it was valuable training – I was flying most days. From Banff I went to Lossiemouth. I was a senior on any course that I embarked on because my year in America meant I had a higher rank. I was a flight lieutenant when I arrived in Lossiemouth and I had a good rating as a pilot – above average.

Reg started at Lossiemouth on 14 September and began the process of forming up his crew, in preparation for operational duties.

My bomb aimer was the first one who approached me. His brother was a flying instructor at Lossiemouth so knew who they thought were pretty good. The bomb aimer was top of his course and I was top of my course so we joined up. We also got a navigator who was the top of the navigator's course.

We were flying Wimpys, Wellingtons, and on one occasion I was asked to take up a flight engineer instructor with one of his pupils. I proceeded to take off and we hadn't reached any sort of height when suddenly both engines cut out. Being well drilled in the procedure as a pilot I knew what action to take. The Duke of Kent was killed in Scotland because he had engine failure on take-off. He made the fatal mistake of banking the aircraft, hopefully to turn back to the airfield. But the moment you bank you lose lift and go straight into the ground. I knew the procedure was to go straight ahead. There is no point in thinking why it is happening because split seconds count. Suddenly you are on your way down towards the ground. Keeping flying speed is important, and dropping the nose and heading down into the trees. Fortunately, there were a lot of trees, and the tops would give us a softer landing than if we were going straight into the trunks or into the ground. However, before we actually hit the trees the engines spluttered back into life. We always took off with the engines drawing fuel from both tanks and at some point after take-off the flight engineer's job was to turn off one tank and draw fuel from the other one until later in the flight, then swap the tanks over and fly back on the other tank. Anyway, what they managed to do between them was to turn off the fuel for both tanks. How it could happen, who knows, but it could have easily been fatal.

Following his time at No. 20 OTU, RAF Lossiemouth, Reg and his crew were posted to No. 1663 Heavy Conversion Unit, to familiarise themselves with four-engined aircraft, arriving there on 9 March 1944.

However, prior to that we had a couple of weeks on a battle course. Anything at all to hold us back until they had found aircraft for us to fly. The crew didn't appreciate this very much – under the control of the Army, crawling under barbed wire with live ammunition being fired ahead of us. They were all delaying tactics to keep us entertained until we could actually get to a bomber station.

On completion of their time at the Heavy Conversion Unit at RAF Rufforth, where the crew converted to Halifaxes, Reg was graded as 'above the average'. On 29 April 1944 they arrived at No. 76 Squadron, RAF Holme-on-Spalding-Moor, close to the Humber.

This proved very useful, as flying back from Germany there was a canal that was very conveniently situated, leading us directly to our airfield. At night water always has some sort of reflection so that was quite valuable. The Halifax was a fine bomber as far as I was concerned. But every aircraft I flew, at any time, was always the best one I had flown. I never had any grievances with any planes at all.

We were a very tightly knit crew and got on well together. Three of us were commissioned. The other four were not – the wireless operator, flight engineer and two gunners – but we all had a very friendly relationship. We lived in separate Messes but we used to meet up together off camp. When we were shot down, of those who survived and became prisoners of war, my NCOs were all in the same compound as me. I was able to meet up with them and see them most days. We were free to walk round the perimeter for exercise, and I could visit them in their room. It was a great thing to be able to socialise with your crew. The only two we could not get together with were the two who had been killed, of course, and the navigator who had broken his leg at the time we were shot down. He was in hospital and was eventually repatriated to Canada.

We formed a very tight bond – and had warm feelings for each other. When you are up in the sky together you all depend on each other. I know people tend to glamorise the pilot but the fact is that the pilot cannot do it all on his own. Everyone in the crew is absolutely indispensable and we all had a very good relationship. I heard once from one pilot who insisted on his crew saluting him because he was commissioned and they weren't. I cannot imagine what sort of relationship that crew had with their skipper – extraordinary.

We didn't have any problems discipline wise. There was one occasion when the wireless operator got a little bit rattled, and the mid-upper, who had already done a tour of operations as a gunner and was a warrant officer, spoke up and said to the particular crew member: 'We have only got one skipper on this aircraft', and that was the end of it. We were happy to be doing what we were doing. We enjoyed each other's company, we enjoyed flying, the more flying we did the better, and lots of flying that was not operational.

When Reg arrived at No. 76 Squadron, Bomber Command had recently undergone a marked change in terms of strategic direction. The campaign against Berlin and other German cities in the winter of 1943 and 1944 had passed with varying degrees of success but at a considerable cost in terms of men and aircraft. Overall, Allied emphasis in western Europe now shifted to preparations for the Normandy D-Day landings. Bomber Command's role included the pre- and post-invasion 'Transportation Plan' – attacking road and rail targets through which German troops and armour would pass to the battlefront. It was a key element in firstly winning a beachhead when the invasion was launched, and then supporting the breakout and advance across France.

Reg took off for his first operational sortie on 10 May 1944, to attack a Transportation Plan target, the railyards at Lens. And over the course of the next few weeks the crew's tally of successful flights over hostile territory accumulated.

I cannot remember being apprehensive. We were always excited. You were excited if you were going into a situation of danger but you relished it too. Otherwise, why did people who had finished their tours go on and do another tour and then an extra one? I never had any feeling that any of my crew were worried or troubled when we were setting off on ops.

Following the raid to Lens, Reg took his crew to Trouville railyards (11/12 May), Bourg-Leopold military camp (27/28 May), Fermé d'Urville enemy radio listening station (1/2 June), and Trappes railyards (2/3 June). On 5 June, Reg and his crew were detailed to attack

the Normandy coastal gun batteries at Mont Fleury early the following morning.

We didn't know when D-Day was going to be and of course we didn't know where it would be. Nobody ever knew anything, except what you were doing yourself on the actual operation you were going on. You didn't know how it formed part of a greater picture. On D-Day, having bombed one hour before dawn, we flew back to Holme-on-Spalding-Moor, were debriefed, and went to bed. At half-past eight in the morning the BBC announced that it was D-Day, but we didn't know anything about it as we got up at lunchtime. The first thing you did, before you had lunch, was to ask the question – Are we on tonight? We found out that we were, it was D-Day, and we had taken a part in it without knowing.

On the evening of 6 June Reg was again operational. 'We were charged with carrying out a daylight operation to bomb the German airfield at Saint-Lô in Normandy.'

To enable me to see our target, because of heavy cloud cover, we had to reduce height to below 3,000 feet. This put us within range of cannon fire from the ground and I could see the tracer shells being directed towards us. Taking action to avoid them I was reminded of being chased around our garden by my father with his garden hose!

I had no difficulty in throwing our Halifax bomber around the sky trying to avoid us being hit, because I had spent a whole year instructing pupils on aerobatics on the Harvard AT6. When a cannon shell hit our aircraft our Halifax was, at that moment, flying at an angle of 90° to the ground. The shell went through the Perspex window of our rear turret and out through the other side without exploding. It made a dinner-plate-size hole in the Perspex on each side of our rear gunner, Desmond Hemmings, known to us as 'Dizzy'. He described seeing a blue flash as the shell passed just in front of his face. Miraculously he was not hurt. When the shell hit us, if we had been flying level instead of 90° to the ground, it would have hit the body of our fuselage and exploded. That would have meant the end of me and my crew.

The following fortnight was taken up with raids in support of the land battle: Juvisy railyards (7/8 June), Laval airfield (9/10 June), Longueau railyards (12/13 June), Douai railyards (14/15 June) and Fouillard ammunition dump (15/16 June). On 19 June Reg was detailed to attack the V-1 flying bomb supply site at Domleger but was recalled and jettisoned his bombs in the North Sea. Clearly Reg and his crew were proving themselves as an adept and effective crew, and thoughts turned towards testing themselves further.

Inspired by our mid-upper, who had already done one tour, the idea of going on to special duties sounded rather attractive and we thought, yes, that would be rather exciting. We had a very good standing as a crew and were highly thought of. Following the very first trip we did at No. 76 Squadron, the bombing photos were up on a big board and ours was the best of them. It gave us quite a lift to think that we did so well. We had an outstanding navigator, Canadian Hannes Vidal, quite outstanding. On trips across Germany, particularly when we were in Pathfinder Force, he used to get a fix and produce a fresh change of course if necessary, or change of speed, every six minutes – now that is a marvel of concentration. Sitting in the aircraft, all hell let loose outside and always with the noise of the engines and the general vibration. But he was so focused he worked out a fresh fix every six minutes. Ten times in an hour and on a three-hour flight, that is thirty times – a lot of work for a navigator to do and he always got us to the right target and always on time.

We applied for special duties and were then sent on leave. The intention was to be posted to Italy and become involved in the Balkans, supporting the partisans under Tito. However, on the last day of our leave we received telegrams telling us to report back to our station. Hamish Mahaddie, the 'poacher' as he was described, interviewed us and we were selected for the Pathfinders. We didn't quarrel with that at all – it was a big promotion.

The gunners were not happy because on the Halifax they had Boulton Paul turrets, which were much more spacious. We now went on to Avro Lancasters and they had Frazer Nash turrets, which they found very cramped. I remember feeling the excitement and the challenge of flying a faster aircraft with a higher ceiling. A beautiful aircraft to fly. But I found no fault with the Halifax at all – the engines never let us down. We had Merlin engines on both the Halifax and the Lancaster so there was no change there. It was a tremendous privilege as far as I was concerned.

Reg and his crew were posted to No. 635 Squadron, RAF Downham Market, arriving on 20 July 1944. Reg flew his first operation to Kiel on 23 July, acting as a second pilot.

I did my first trip as a second dickey and that was my least enjoyable flight – sitting there not doing anything but watching all this flak coming up in the searchlights. And the pilot sitting beside me flying the aeroplane. It was a waste of time. I can't remember that I learned anything from the flight because I knew what searchlights looked like, and I knew what flak looked like. We had already seen plenty while flying in the main force. I did my second dickey with Flight Lieutenant Wheble. A month later we went to Kiel again with our separate crews in our separate aircraft and we both got shot down.

Wheble's navigator was a squadron leader so he must have done an awful lot of operations. Years later my wife and I went to a reunion in Downham Market to unveil a memorial to the Victoria Crosses that had been awarded at the station. We met up with the widow of the navigator who had flown with me on my second dickey trip, and who had had three children – all under five – when he was killed. He ought not to have been flying. We were not that short of navigators that we couldn't manage without him I am sure, but there it is. I think that aircrew tended to want to go on and on and on until they didn't make it. My wife and I always kept in touch with his family. I still hear from the daughter who was only three when her father was killed, and went with her mother to receive her father's Distinguished Flying Cross from King George at Buckingham Palace. She writes often and she always sends me a card with a Lancaster on the front.

On 27 July Reg, as sole pilot, carried out a daylight raid to the V-1 site at Les Haut Boissons. Following a night attack on Hamburg, Reg then carried out three further daylight raids, attacking enemy troop positions south-east of Caumont and near Falaise on 30 July and

14 August respectively, with a bombardment of the V-weapon site at Trossy St Maximin on 4 August. 'It was an incredible experience seeing the sky full of aircraft.' At night the shroud of darkness isolated the crew somewhat, although on one raid Reg recalled 'the bomb aimer pointing out that there was an aircraft above us just a little bit to the left. It is the only time I can remember seeing an aircraft really close because, in the darkness, we kept all our cockpit and instrument lights turned right down as low as possible.' Reg also recalls seeing one aircraft coned by searchlights on a night raid: 'We suddenly saw them explode, just like that and that was the end of them.' On 16 August the Barker crew prepared for another sortie deep into Germany.

Stettin was the furthest target we went to. Quite a long trip and I got awfully stiff legs sitting in the seat for about seven and a half hours. We had a failure of our super charger and we couldn't reach the intended height. The only way to try and maintain our timing – it was always very important to be on time – was to use any height that we could obtain, then put our nose down a bit and increase our speed. We bombed at 9,000 feet and on that particular occasion no searchlights attacked us at that height. If they had we might have been seriously coned and that would have been the end of us. We didn't have any flak at all. It was all above us, thousands of feet above us – all the flak, all the searchlights, all the activity was up there. We thought this was great but we didn't think at the time of the bombs that were dropping on us. We got back and decided to fly to Woodbridge, which was an emergency field several miles long. Being cautious I put the aircraft down just over the edge and we had to taxi mile after mile after mile following the vehicle that said 'follow me'. That was an incident that turned out happily.

There was another occasion when we did see flak ahead of us. We were coming back from an op, routed over Gravesend on the River Thames, and as were flying over the coast we saw flak bursting ahead of us. Well, I mean the first instinct you have is that we must be flying in the wrong direction – but we weren't. After thinking that we needed to do something about this, I climbed well above it, but another of our squadron's aircraft was absolutely peppered, and we believe that it was the guns firing at the V-1s over the Thames. It is a bit perplexing when you see flak coming up in your own country – you do wonder what is happening.

Following the Stettin attack, Reg next took part in a raid on Bremen two nights later. It was just over a week before he would next be operational. Accompanying Reg was his navigator Hannes Vidal, bomb aimer Brian Boston, wireless operator 'Dick' Bird, mid-upper gunner 'Taffy' Kinsey, rear gunner 'Dizzy' Hemmings and flight engineer Harry Bullock.

The Allies were making great progress across France. Paris had been liberated and we thought the war was not going to last much longer – another three weeks or so and it could be over. We were on our way to the Rhine and good old Monty would be sorting them out in due course.

Chapter Twelve

I Was Going to Die

On 26 August our target was Kiel, a very important naval base for the Germans. That was where they were launching their submarines against the Allied navies that were crossing the Channel. The armies we had in France depended on the ships to maintain supplies of ammunition and food. Everything rested on the ships safely traversing the Channel and they were vulnerable to U-boats. We bombed Kiel dead on time, thanks to our amazing navigator. The gunners and the wireless operator were searching the sky looking out for fighters. We had left the flak and searchlights behind but suddenly there was a tremendous explosion and the aircraft was turned on its back. I managed to right the aircraft and called up each member of the crew to check they were all okay, which they were – they all responded. But we had a fire in the starboard wing. Only that week I had read of a crew who had managed to blow the fire out by putting the aircraft into a shallow dive and increasing speed, which I did. But almost immediately – as I was holding the control column, of course – the nose started going down and I realised I had no control over the tailplane at all. It meant that we had no choice but to abandon the aircraft and I gave the order to the crew. The nose now was right down and we found ourselves in a very tight spin, going vertically back towards the fires of Kiel. My last view of the altimeter – we had been flying at 17,000 feet – showed us to be at 13,000 feet and we were going down at great speed. The moment we were hit I had opened up all four engines to the maximum speed, four beautiful Rolls-Royce Merlin engines. They were behaving perfectly and now we were flying vertically downwards towards the ground. We were only seconds away from death. The G force was so great that I was lifted out of my seat and I was aware that there was no alternative but to hit the ground. I remember a momentary prayer – God make it quick. I didn't really want to be fried up in the fires. This was split seconds we were talking about. There wasn't any time for my life to pass before me.

The moment I had given the order to 'abandon aircraft' the bomb aimer, who was down in the nose, opened the hatch and dropped out. With the hatch open there was a terrific roaring of wind through the plane. We were descending at this tremendous speed and it was absolutely deafening. I had never, ever heard such a loud shrieking noise – four Rolls-Royce Merlin engines screaming away, the aircraft vibrating, and the noise of the wind blowing through. I didn't know at that time that we had lost our tail and that was why we were in this vertical spin. So this was the end of Reggie Barker. I felt so at peace; it was an incredible feeling of calmness after knowing that certainly I was going to die. This was the end of my life, there was no question about it and it didn't panic me in any way at all. The end was here and that was it.

Suddenly, after this most deafening noise there was total silence. I blacked out. I lost vision, lost hearing, everything was silent. Total silence. Reggie Barker had arrived in that heavenly place to which he was obviously intended. But after a few moments of this amazing quietness, total bliss, this peace, suddenly there came this swishing sound, which I later realised was the wind tearing through my clothes as I was hurtling towards the ground. I was outside the aircraft. I was exposed to the cold night air. Then my vision came back and there beside me, careering towards the earth, was my blazing aircraft. I realised I was in the sky and instinctively my right hand went to the ripcord to pull it, but I hadn't got any feeling in my right hand. I put my left hand on it, pulled my glove off and with my left hand pushed my right hand to pull away at the D ring and release the parachute. At that moment, I saw the tree tops brilliantly illuminated by the fire from my aircraft. I dropped into the trees and hung there for a moment. I thought I had better not stay there, this was not a very good place to be, I had better get myself down. I managed to undo whatever it was that held me to the parachute and clambered down through the branches, which eventually gave out so I put my arms tightly around the trunk of this tree and then dropped softly on to a thick carpet of leaves. I looked up at the night sky and there was the polar star. Very useful because I knew then that I wasn't very many miles from the Danish border.

My instinct was to get to Denmark because that was where I could find help. I set off and when I got to the edge of the wood I had to think of what to do next. I knew the direction I wanted to go and began crawling along a ditch. I suddenly became aware of voices and then people approaching me. They must have seen me silhouetted against the fire, as the trees were on fire, not just the aeroplane. Someone said, in German, something like 'Come with me.' It sounded friendly enough. I became surrounded. There weren't any middle-aged men. They were either very old or very young. They all grabbed part of my battledress. The children were holding on to my trousers, all clinging terribly tightly to this British RAF Terrorflieger as they called me. To my mind, how could I be a Terrorflieger? I was here to liberate them, to liberate Europe from the Nazis. Things are very much black and white when you are young and in that situation. All these people were so excited. They had heard my aircraft screaming down over their village doing hundreds and hundreds of miles an hour – it must have made a tremendous din. They must have been terrified out of their lives. And then they captured the Terrorflieger, so what were they to do with him? A teenager held a revolver of some kind, a small pistol, which he had up at my head. His hand was shaking. And there was I completely consumed with calmness. I felt sorry for these people really, it was an extraordinary situation.

After a little while, they handed me over to two men in uniform. I had to accompany them with hands on my head and they gave me the odd kick but nothing more. They marched me to a farmhouse where I was taken up to the first floor. Looking out through the window all I could see was a big farmyard. It was a huge glass-plate window and I thought of jumping through like Errol Flynn, who was one of our cinema heroes. But I was never left alone, of course, there was always a guard with me in the room. They used to change over every few hours and would love to play with their revolver, thinking if only this chap would take a running jump through the window. It didn't happen because I decided that I wasn't Errol Flynn and the plate-glass window wasn't, like in the films, made of sugar. A young girl brought in a jug of some sort of gruel. I didn't have any appetite – I must have been in shock. After some time I was taken downstairs to use the toilet, which they were always very considerate about, and I recognised, from something that was on it, a battledress that belonged to my rear gunner.

We were shot down on the Saturday night, and on the Sunday night I was taken down to some men in navy blue uniforms. I was put on a horse-drawn hay cart and there to my amazement was my rear gunner Dizzy, and also my navigator Hannes who had broken his leg. He was transferred to hospital and I was taken to an airfield and put in a cell. Through a small opening – there wasn't a proper window but a little barred hole in the wall – I could see Heinkel IIIs on the airfield. Extraordinary, I had never seen a Heinkel III before, and there was a row of them on this airfield. It was all like living through a cinema reel. I remember tapping messages on the wall, between myself and someone from Flight Lieutenant Wheble's crew on the other side. It couldn't amount to anything. There was no way we could escape.

Eventually I was taken to Hamburg. With other POWs we were marched along a street, and either side were huge piles of rubble. No buildings, just rubble heaped very, very high, until we came to the only building standing, which was obviously a very old gaol. We went down staircases and through heavy doors and it reminded me of a film about the Count of Monte Cristo; it all seemed black and white. We ended up on a cobbled floor, a very damp cobbled floor, with a bucket in the corner. We were stripped at some point, but then given our clothes back.

The next day Reg was transported by train to Frankfurt. 'There were about four of us in the compartment with a German who said, "It's no good."' Reg eventually arrived at Dulag Luft transit camp for interrogation and processing, 'and we were put in solitary confinement for five days'.

I had various interrogations. I never needed to give more than my name, rank and number. One was pressed with various types of approach. There was a friendly man who had been to Cambridge, well educated, and he talked about the difficulties Germany faced after the First World War. I suppose this was to arouse sympathy and then hope that he could get some information, but it didn't work. In my case I was just naïve, and as far as I was concerned just name, rank and number was all I was able to give. Then there were the bully boys – they were aggressive – but they didn't actually harm you in any way. But they made me realise how tough they could be if they wanted to, if I didn't cooperate, which I didn't of course. And then there was the bogus Red Cross form. It all looked very official. There were lots of questions, starting off with name, rank and number and then parents' names, and religions, place of birth, etc. and then it got more detailed. Naturally, they wanted to know about the squadron you flew in, the operations that you were on, the aircraft that you were flying, etc. The danger was that if you just filled in name, rank, and number they might then fill in the rest and take it to the members of your crew and say, 'Look, your skipper's filled it in.' So, I put lines through all the questions that I didn't want to answer. They ranted and raved – they didn't like that. It all sounds like something of a game. I was twenty-two and I was alive, and they were losing the war. Any day I would be home. I judged within a week, maybe three weeks, but I was proved a bit out.

Eventually we were all assembled, about fifty of us, and because I was the senior officer I was asked to stand in front of the parade and instruct my comrades that we would give the Germans an assurance that we would not make any attempt to escape on the journey to wherever we were going. I turned and faced them all and said, 'Well, you hear what they say chaps. They want us to promise that we won't try to escape. But we all know that if we have the opportunity to escape it is what we want to do, and it is our duty anyway.' I turned back to our captors and they weren't very happy about this. They then decided we would all have our boots removed when we got on the train. We travelled all the way across from Frankfurt am Main to Frankfurt an der Oder and then turned north, all the way up to Stettin. Then we bore west and ended up at Barth on the Baltic Sea, and Stalag Luft I.

Reg, along with four of his crew had survived the ordeal of being shot down, parachuting to earth, and were placed in captivity. Two of Reg's crew did not survive. In later life Reg wrote down his thoughts in regard to the fate of his crew following the combat on 26 August 1944.

For the five of us who survived, our greatest sorrow has been the loss of two members of our crew: Brian Boston, our bomb aimer, and Taffy Kinsey, our mid-upper gunner. Both of them are buried in Kiel War Cemetery. Brian was the only crew member who had time to bale out through the forward escape hatch. It was just after he jumped that the aircraft made its violent nose-dive. We believe he must have been struck by some part of the aircraft and been knocked unconscious, for he was found in a field with his parachute unopened. Taffy was reported to have died in the aircraft. Once it started its uncontrolled dive it would have been impossible for him to extricate himself from his cramped turret. Like those of us in the forward section of the aircraft he would have been trapped, as we were, by the irresistible force of G. After blacking out, he could have known nothing more.

The pain of losing those two comrades, both fine young men in their twenties, has remained with me all my life. Scarcely a day passes when I do not remember them.

Among Reg's archive of documents are a bundle of letters written to and from his father in correspondence with the family members of Reg's crew following their loss. Some of these make extremely sad reading, reflecting the weight of anxiety they were all experiencing.

To Edith Bullock (flight engineer Harry Bullock's wife) from John Barker, 23 September.

It is certainly not a very appropriate time for making new friendships and yet I feel as parent of the crew's pilot (F/Lt Reg Barker) that I would like to offer my sympathies and hopes to you as wife of the flight engineer. I received your address from Mrs Bird for although I knew the names of the crew I had no addresses and to ask for some would have been seeking contempt. Reg was a very capable pilot and I have great faith in his being able to land his ship if there was the least possibility. I have watched the forming of the crew from the beginning and they had great faith in themselves and in one another and I am sure none would have wished to be 'out' when briefed for that most dangerous mission; where the ack ack is so intense that they can only fly through it and take their chance. So I think we can only do them justice by having faith in them and living in hope of receiving better news in the future. Mrs Barker and myself send you our kindest regards and best wishes.

From Edith Bullock to John Barker, 4 October.
I feel as if I must write to you, after receiving such wonderful news, that I have heard that my husband is a prisoner of war in Germany, and pray that the rest of the crew are safe with him. A Mrs Merryfield, quite unknown to me, heard the news from a German broadcast. Of course I would not build my hopes too high, then a reporter from the local paper called on me showing me a message that Harold had sent to me saying that he was safe and well. I was so excited I could hardly believe it.

I called on the lady yesterday evening thanking her for sending the good news and asking if she could remember any other names that had been given out. I could name all the crew but one and that was the mid-upper gunner, whom I have only heard of as 'Taffy'. As soon as I mentioned Hemmings of Breconshire, she immediately said, 'I am sure that name was given out tonight' (Tues), and in that message it said they were all safe and well, all but Frank, who was killed; of course, she might easily have been mixed up with another name, but I do hope and pray they are all safe, only one has to be so careful over these broadcasts.

When I arrived home much later a telegram from the Air Ministry awaited me, saying that the name of my husband was included in a German broadcast, but as yet I have had no official information. Hoping you also have received good news.

When John Barker wrote to Mr Kinsey, Bill Kinsey's father, in October, he had heard that Reg was also safe. On 11 October Mr Kinsey replied.
I was very glad to have your letter today and to know you have heard that the skipper is safe. I have no information this way since the notification. I hope and trust the Germans' news is true. Somehow I have a feeling that the crew are all safe. Just a hunch that's all. On the night of Aug 26/27 I was downstairs, as is my custom, until about 2 a.m. At 1.30 I 'felt' that Bill was in trouble, and although I would naturally have been relieved I would have been surprised if the telegraph boy

didn't appear on Mon. morning. Worse luck he did, but after the first awful few moments I felt as I have said, as Bill had done in the neighbourhood of 60 ops over Germany his luck was very good. Now we are left with the hope that our lads will one day cross the threshold again. Should I hear anything definite I will lose no time in writing you.

On 5 December 1944, Mr Kinsey wrote to John Barker again.
I have heard from the Air Ministry. They say five of the crew are POWs in Germany and two lost their lives. Flying Officer Dobson (sic) and one unidentified as yet. That was Bill my son. It will be a miracle if such is not the case. I must not complain. Thousands have had to sacrifice so that future generations may live in freedom.

One thing comforts me above all else on this earth. Bill (or 'Taffy' as the RAF knew him) was in the job he wanted from childhood. That is the fortune of war. I had a family. Wife, two sons and one daughter in September 1941, and (except for my son John who is in the States since 1937) I am all alone. But I have very happy memories that always remain. I must say my son's luck was phenomenal. He had done around 60 ops.

Well Mr Barker, I am glad you know your son is safe. Perhaps at some future date I may be able to hear or read some details of their last op on the 26/27 Aug. I sometimes think Dobson and Bill were either killed or wounded by flak and were unable to bail out. Let us all earnestly hope and pray that this awful business will soon end, and that the war will definitely ensure peace for a long time to come.

On 24 January, John Barker replied to Mr Kinsey.
Many times since receiving your letter I have tried to write to you but the words will just not come to me. Your news was a great shock to me for I had hoped and prayed for something better. Then I awaited a letter from my Son hoping it would give me some help. But it brought no information about that unfortunate flight. I felt I had known Taffy so well, although we had never met, for I had followed the forming of the crew and their subsequent progress with great interest. It certainly does you great credit in the way you try to console yourself and I admire your spirit yet know that inwardly you must feel that deep irreplaceable

loss. This after your other losses must have been a bitter blow and my heart and understanding go out to you. It is with this understanding that I realise how futile it is to try and express one's feelings on paper. Perhaps someday we shall have the pleasure of talking things over with more facts before us than we have at present.

I have tried my best to express myself and yet it seems but a very poor effort, but I trust that this will at least dispel any bad thoughts you may have had by not hearing from me earlier.

By the time Reg arrived at Stalag Luft I at Barth, on the Baltic coast, the camp had been hosting fallen airmen for over five years. The number of compounds and occupants had steadily grown over the course of the war, and there had been various purges to and from other camps as the Germans tried to manage the increasing numbers of POWs. It was now September 1944 and Reg, finding himself incarcerated behind barbed wire, felt no diminishing of his morale.

We expected the war to be over very soon. We were on the winning side. It was exciting to arrive in the camp and have a proper bed and not be in the train. We had been twelve to a compartment. Sometimes we would sleep in the luggage rack but otherwise we slept on the floor or along the corridor. It wasn't a very comfortable journey and we didn't get very much to eat. On the first night in camp I was put in a room that had mould. It had been there for a very long time and there was an Army doctor who we thought was mad. Everybody thought he was mad – he had this ridiculous idea that the war would not be over until Easter 1945.

We did receive orders from the senior officer that no more escapes were allowed. I think this probably resulted from the murder of the fifty who had escaped from Stalag Luft III in March 1944. It wasn't considered sensible to organise any more mass escapes. The war was so near the end, as we believed, that it was pointless really.

While a prisoner Reg kept an exercise book in which he transcribed poetry by fellow POWs and the more well-known classic poets. Also he noted down an extensive list of the books and essays that he read, alongside which he studied mathematics. He also took the

opportunity to write home, detailing some aspects of his day to day life and also his continual optimism of a quick homecoming. Florrie, mentioned in his letters, was his father's new wife Florence Way, Gerald was his brother, Eileen his sister ('E' in one of the letters), and Will was Florrie's brother William Way who had been killed in action (Flight Lieutenant William Way, DFC, lost his life in a No. 35 Squadron Halifax on the 5/6 January 1944 raid to Stettin). Monica is a female acquaintance of Reg's at the time.

16 September 1944
Dear Dad, Florrie and Gerald. Well at last I am able to write you a proper letter and to tell you that I'm quite well and finding life here quite tolerable – especially as we all feel that it will only be a few weeks before we shall be on our way home again. I'm now at a permanent camp and have been busy 'settling in'. We've been scrubbing out our quarters and generally trying to get things ship-shape. I am getting heaps of fresh air and sunshine now that I am in a proper camp, so that I am getting some of my old colour back again. Hannes is in hospital but will be OK. Dick, Dizzy and Harry are here with me. Thanks to the Red Cross – they do a wonderful job here – we eat reasonably well. And so far I am finding plenty to keep me occupied. Am writing to Monica and E. Love to yourselves, Granma and all. Keep well, Affectionately, Reg.

28 September 1944
Dear Dad, Florrie and Gerald. Am I too optimistic in doubting whether you will receive this card before you have the pleasure of seeing me? I hope not! I am quite well and am getting through a lot of books – my latest a biography of Edgar Wallace. Some of the boys are putting on a play tomorrow. Should be fun. Eager as ever for the day of liberation. Hope you all are well. Love, Reg

19 October 1944
Dear Dad, Florrie and Gerald. I like to think that you will not receive these letters of mine until well after I get home. If the news continues as good as it is now there won't be much doubt about it! But writing to

you makes me feel much closer to home, which naturally seems a long way off in these strange surroundings. Surprisingly the days seem to pass quite quickly, although most of our time is leisure time. I have never yet been bored for there are so many interesting books here to read, so many interesting topics to discuss. There are Canadians, South Africans, Irish and Englishmen in my room, so we never lack for something to argue about! Potatoes form the bulk of our food, and because they are so fattening I am actually filling out! Also I have a tache so you probably won't recognise me. I wonder whether you know yet that I am a prisoner – that has been my big worry since I was shot down – the knowledge that you did not know I was safe. I have prayed many times that somehow you might know. My love and best wishes to you all. Your affectionate son, Reg.

30 October 1944

Dear Dad, Florrie, Eileen and Gerald. By the time that you get my letter it will be nearly Xmas, so just in case (!) I send you all my best wishes that you may spend it happily and together. And because I'm still optimistic I also say that I hope to spend it with you! I'm longing to be home – need I say? But meanwhile I'm making the most of this fine opportunity for study. I suppose I shall never have so much time to myself again. I attend classes in Advanced French and Maths, and am studying History and other subjects on my own. With lots of general reading you can imagine how quickly the time passes considering. That of course is one of my chief interests. Yes I'm longing to be back, but I can't help feeling how fortunate I am in only losing 3 or 4 months of my life. Will and so many others gave their all. I was spared that. I am perfectly fit and thanks as ever to the Red Cross, am still eating reasonably well. There should be some letters for me in a couple of weeks. How I am looking forward to them. Dinner's being served up. Stew I think – smells good!! Cheerio for now. My love to you all. Affectionately, Reg.

20 November 1944

Dear Dad, Florrie and Gerald. Well at last the big offensive on the West Front has opened up. We are following all the news bulletins very closely and there is an atmosphere of eager anticipation in the camp. Shall we be home for Xmas? That is what is on most people's minds. If the weather is favourable I believe we can. 'Hope springs eternal in the human breast.' In a prison camp one lives on hope! Nothing changes here very much, except of course the weather. More and more often our time has to be spent indoors. That means fewer outdoor games and more reading. One result of this is that I've developed a taste for good books, which I hope to carry with me through later years. In a sense of course one's only contact with the outside world is through the medium of books, hence I read, besides the classics and poetry etc., books of modern travel and adventure. Of course they increase one's already almost insane desire to be the other side of the barbed wire. But if that prevents one sinking into a state of resignation it's a good thing! I do hope you all had a good Xmas and saved me a piece of pudding. Keep well – all my love to all. Your affectionate son, Reg.

17 January 1945

Dear Dad, Florrie and Gerald. So 1945 is here and with it renewed hopes for our return. We saw the New Year in and what a welcome we gave it! Now Joe is on the move and our spirits are high even though the food situation has deteriorated considerably recently. We are not receiving any Red Cross parcels at the moment and the German food doesn't amount to very much. But don't worry, we get along and how we shall enjoy our food when we get home. Most nights I dream that I am at home with yourselves, or with Monica, but food always plays a big part too! Dizzy has just received 2 letters. His latest is dated the middle of November, so I have hopes of hearing soon. I gather his people were informed by radio whereas you presumably had to wait for my first letter to arrive. Dick, Dizzy and Harry are quite well. Hannes hasn't turned up here so I presume that when he left hospital he was sent to another camp and if you are able to write to him please send best wishes from us all here. I often think of [...] Maisey and wonder how he is getting on. I still do heaps of reading, and just starting 'Vanity Fair', but am looking forward to better weather when I can spend more time outside. I hope you are all well and send you my fondest love. Your affectionate son, Reg.

In April 1945 it became clear to the inmates at Barth, and their captors, that the Russian Army would soon be upon them. Group Captain C.T. 'Ginger' Weir and the senior Allied officer Colonel Hub Zemke, USAAF, met with the camp commandant who showed them a message received from the Oberkommando der Wehrmacht – the German High Command. Zemke recalled: 'What I heard set my hair on end. The gist of the message was that all German personnel and prisoners of war were to be ready to evacuate Stalag Luft I within 24 hours, moving to an undesignated location in the Hamburg area.' The Allied senior officers' response was that they were having none of it, a calculated but risky gamble that was passed back to OKW. A short time later, in the early hours of 30 April 1945 and with no response from the High Command, the Germans at Stalag Luft I informed Zemke and Weir that they would peacefully depart the camp in the next few hours. On the first day of May 1945, Colonel Zemke took charge at Stalag Luft I.[5]

When the Germans left, and before the Russians reached us, they handed over the gun positions to our own chaps. Our senior officers knew which of us had handled rifles. Maybe some of them might have been in the Army – they came out at Dunkirk and decided to join the RAF instead. It was quite a surprise to find our own chaps up manning the guns in the gun towers.

Suddenly, there was a murmur on 1 May 1945. We had a sense of some excitement and it almost seemed as if the ground was rumbling and trembling. Hundreds of POWs, thousands perhaps, were racing across the sandy compound towards the fence and the gate where the Russians had arrived. It was so exhilarating and quite extraordinary. We received orders from our senior officers that we must not leave the camp. They were concerned about us going off and getting beaten up or maybe shot by marauding German soldiers. But they relented after a day or two. I rather think a Russian drew a pistol on one of the senior officers, and opened the gates and left them open.

We wandered down into the local town, which was rather boring because there were no people around. Instead, there were white flags hanging out of the windows. People in that locality must have been terrified of the

Russians – I think they were pretty brutal. We waited patiently to be brought back to England but in the meantime the Russians issued us with four Red Cross parcels. Between the August when I had been captured and Christmas we had received one Red Cross parcel per man per week. Otherwise the German ration was one loaf of black bread and a bowl of potato soup each day. From Christmas 1944 until May 1945, when we were liberated, we were reduced to the bare German rations, which was one loaf of black bread per week per man and one bowl of potato soup. We did, in fact, manage to supplement our rations because we discovered that after the potatoes had been peeled the peelings went down a chute into a bin where they were collected by a local farmer to feed his pigs. We thought we were more worthy than the pigs so we used to scuttle along underneath the windows, out of sight, and fill a bowl with these potato peelings, and take them back and boil them up.

After we were liberated I recall seeing one of the poor devils from a local concentration camp squatting on the sand fairly near the entrance. The doctor had been attending him but was warning us to keep away from him because of disease. He could not be given anything to eat because it was reckoned it would kill him if he was given a proper meal. He had the black and white pyjamas they were provided with in those terrible concentration camps. That wasn't a very happy scene.

Anyway, the Russians broke open the Red Cross store and gave us each four Red Cross parcels, which would have been equivalent to a month's rations during the days before Christmas. But not having received any parcels from Christmas until 1 May, when they did arrive from then on it seemed like Christmas. I remember making toffee with the powdered milk and the sugar.

We were held for twelve days but it didn't bother us; we knew that it was just a matter of waiting to be flown out. It was only years later that I learned that we were actually held as hostages by the Russians – they wouldn't allow us to go. The Americans had the aircraft all lined up at an airfield not very far away but the Americans had apparently captured a Russian general along with his army, who had gone over to their side at some point during the war. Evidently the Russians had heard of this and they demanded that this Russian general be handed over to them. It took time to organise and it wasn't until the day he was actually handed over – I read later – that the Russians gave the order for us to be released. In due course we were marched away from our camp and taken to an airfield. I took my seat in a Flying Fortress, so I had the distinction of flying there in a Lancaster and flying home in an American B-17. I always wondered afterwards if the pilot might have been one of my cadets from my days as an instructor. We were packed tightly into the aeroplane, but very pleased to arrive back home in England, with the green grass and middle-aged ladies of the Women's Voluntary Service greeting us with cups of tea and sandwiches. We were back in Blighty.

After what must have been an emotional reunion with his family, and some leave, Reg soon found his services were once more needed by the RAF. 'I was sent to Transport Command.'

Aircraft were moving troops all over the place and I was sent to Membury, and then dispatched on a Traffic Officer course all about passengers and freight. The idea was that they had to have a section on each station where freight, newspapers and mail were handled backwards and forwards to Germany. We had a big Army in Germany who had to be supplied and there were the prisoners of war out in the Far East to be brought back. When the war ended a lot of those POWs were in such poor shape physically that they spent months in hospital before they could come back to this country. After this course I was posted to be senior traffic officer in charge of the passenger and freight section at an RAF station in Somerset called Merryfield. There was a WAAF officer there in the intelligence section, Joan. With the war over they no longer needed intelligence officers, so they closed the section and Joan was posted to my section. She was the girl I married.

Reg and Joan had two children, Clare and Sylvia, four grandchildren, and at time of writing six great-grandchildren with one on the way. Sadly, Joan passed away in 2008. At the time of putting this book together, Reg was nearing his ninety-sixth birthday. It has been a pleasure to spend time with him over recent years and be able to go through his archive. I hope through this story the reader has been able to get a feel for Reg's nature. A wonderful man, with an

infectious bonhomie and air of goodwill. However, I do get the distinct impression that Reg still battles demons in regard to what happened all those years ago on the night of 26/27 August 1944. He will remember the friends he lost, but his optimism of life shines through. In the exercise book that Reg had with him while in captivity is the following unassigned poem, which was written on the wall of a solitary confinement cell in Dulag Luft, Frankfurt, Germany:

It's easy to be nice boys
When everything's OK.
It's easy to be cheerful
When you're having things your way.
But can you hold your head up
And take it on the chin,
When your heart is nearly breaking,
And you feel like giving in?

It was easy back in England
Amongst your friends and folks;
But now you'll miss the friendly hand,
The joy, the songs and jokes.
The road ahead is stony
And unless you're strong in mind.
You'll find it isn't long before
You're lagging far behind.

You've got to climb that hill boys –
It's no use turning back.
There's only one way home
And that's off the beaten track.
Remember that you're British, and
That when you reach the crest,
You'll see a valley cool and green –
England, at her best!

You know there is a saying
That sunshine follows rain –
And sure enough you'll realise
That joy will follow pain.
Let courage be your password
And fortitude your guide;
And then instead of grousing
Just remember those who died!

1	2	3	4	5	6	6	7	8	9	10	11	12	13	14	15

Name:

Henry Wagner

Bomber Command Navigator
Failed to Return from a 17/18 December 1944 Raid to Duisburg

Chapter Thirteen

The War Came

Henry Wagner was born to an Irish mother and father on 24 March 1923, 'although later in life I took out naturalisation papers to become a British citizen', and at the age of three Henry moved to England – Sonning Common, near Reading. His father abandoned the family two years later and his mother was left to bring up her four sons alone. At the age of seven Henry moved to Henley-on-Thames, starting at Henley Grammar School in September 1934. In addition to his academic education, Henry developed a keen interest in golf, a natural talent for Rugby, and 'I soon realised that the languages were my strong point, not the sciences.'

In September 1939 the war came. It was not unexpected but to us boys it did not mean a great deal. We expected it to be over quite quickly, never dreaming that we would become embroiled in it ourselves in the fullness of time. Preparations had been going on for some time in the past – gas masks had been issued, and evacuees came from London, and to our horror stooped so low as to dig in the bunkers on the golf course as if they were on the beach.

On Sunday 3 September we listened to the sad announcement by the Prime Minister Neville Chamberlain on the radio (or wireless as it was called then) at 11am. Shortly afterward the air-raid sirens sounded, and gas masks were brought to the ready – nobody knew what to expect. It was a false alarm, though, and soon afterward we settled down to our Sunday dinner. Then Richard, my younger brother, and I set off over the golf course. It was completely deserted except for us two. At one tee, adjoining the road, we were taken to task and heartily condemned by a passer-by for indulging in a frivolous pursuit at a time of national catastrophe, but it is difficult to see how we could have helped by staying at home.

In 1940, with his schooldays now completed, Henry decided to go into higher education with a view to become a teacher, and he was accepted for Reading University.

At the university the men all enrolled in the Officers' Training Corps with a view to joining the Army. This was not at all to my liking, but I signed up because everybody else did. Wednesday afternoons were given over to training, wearing Army uniform, and consisted of drill, weapon training, tactical exercises, etc., under the supervision of Captain Gillett and Sergeant Major Warwick. After a few months, an Air Training Corps was started, and I thankfully transferred to that. Flying had always been a great interest of mine, and the ATC was much more to my liking. The commanding officer was Professor Miller, with the rank of squadron leader, but he knew little about the Royal Air Force. All the administration was done by a regular RAF officer, Flight Lieutenant Jordan. He had been shot down in a Hurricane and was badly burned about the face. He was assisted by Sergeant Linton, a wireless operator/air gunner, who had been shot down in the desert and had walked back to his own lines. He mounted a Vickers gas-operated machine gun in the grounds, and always manned it when the sirens went, hoping for a crack at a low-flying German aircraft.

As I said, flying had always interested me, and I had my first flight five years before the war began. It was just a matter of good luck, as paying for a flight was obviously not on. Sir Alan Cobham's air circus was due to come to Henley in 1934, and by way of publicity coupons were printed in the Henley Standard, the first ten to be drawn out to be awarded a free flight. I went round all the houses in the neighbourhood asking if I could have their coupons, and sent in a whole batch. One of them brought home the bacon. The flight was in an Armstrong-Whitworth biplane, which seated about twelve people, and lasted for some twenty minutes, over and around Henley. The next flights were undertaken when I was in the University Air Squadron. Flight Lieutenant Jordan used to put up a list in the week of those wanting to fly on Sunday afternoon. He allocated the flights as equally as possible. We flew in various two-seater Miles aircraft from Woodley aerodrome.

In June 1942 Henry took his first-year finals, 'and reached an acceptable standard, studying French with subsidiary Latin. This left one more year to complete the degree course, but there I had to leave it.'

Towards the end of August 1942 my call-up papers arrived and I duly reported to the Aircrew Reception Centre (ACRC, known as Arsy-tarsy) at St John's Wood in London. After a medical along with other members of the University Air Squadron, we were moved to a big block of what were before the war luxury flats (although by then there was not much that was luxurious about them) called Viceroy Court, at Regent's Park, to await events. It was the normal practice for prospective aircrew to be sent to an Initial Training Wing, but since we had done our initial training in the University Air Squadron we were spared that and went straight to a holding unit at Brighton, where we were billeted in the Metropole Hotel right on the front, a building that had been taken over by the Royal Air Force for the duration.

People say to me sometime:, 'Why did you join up? You were of Irish nationality and therefore not under any obligation.' But I felt that this was now my country, and that the obligation did exist. Then they say: 'Well, why volunteer for aircrew then?' But the adventure of flying always enticed me. I felt that that was a job I could do as well as the next man, and that therefore there was no excuse for chickening out. Admittedly, there was not much chance of coming safely out at the other end, but that's the way the cookie crumbles.

After a fortnight or so, postings came through to various grading schools. These were Elementary Flying Training Schools where prospective pilots or navigators were given a twelve-hour course on Tiger Moths. Most were hoping to be pilots, of course, but instructors decided on suitability. I went to Brough, near Hull, and came under the instruction of Flying Officer Rathbone (later killed when a pupil landed a Tiger Moth on top of the one he was taking off in.) I went solo after nine and three-quarter hours, about the average time, and was graded as a pupil pilot.

From Brough I went on leave and then back to Brighton again, this time billeted in the Grand Hotel. The stint there was spent in drill, PT, signals, aircraft recognition, navigation, armament and clay-pigeon shooting. After some weeks there we were warned of imminent posting, and one night left Brighton on a special train that drew out at 2.30am, arriving at Heaton Park, Manchester, at 11am. Heaton Park was where those on overseas postings awaited their draft to a ship, and was a miserable hanging-about restless sort of place. Manchester is a rainy location anyway, and this was in January 1943. It was usually fog-bound and gloomy, and I was in a billet in Salford, some miles from the camp, in a damp, dingy tenement. Thankfully I was not there long before my draft came through, and proceeded by train to Blackpool. All those on draft were dispersed round boarding houses with typical seaside landladies. Tropical kit was issued, so we knew we were off somewhere warm. Three kit bags had to have numbers and names put on in Indian ink – ordinary, flying and tropical.

The time at Blackpool was spent just hanging about waiting – attending lectures, drill, route marches, going to the cinema, and that sort of thing. Finally, after about three weeks, towards the end of February, orders came to move. We went by train to Liverpool, marched to the docks and embarked on a troopship, the SS *Strathmore*, 23,000 tons, and got organised on board, initiated into the process of slinging hammocks. These were hung from bars in the ceiling and were difficult to get into because they were inclined to throw you out again. Also the bars were too close together, with the result that your head was looking directly across at your feet. I soon gave up hammock slinging, and laid mine out on the floor, but I was on the lowest deck of all, below the waterline, and one of the propeller shafts ran just under the floor and thump-thumped away all night, so sleeping was not the rest it should have been. The next day the ship set sail from the Mersey and headed out round the north of Ireland. The sea was green and rough; almost everyone was seasick, and the evening meal was tripe and onions swimming in milk. There were not many takers.

Life on board was pretty leisurely – there were a few lectures, frequent action-stations practice, but most of the time was spent reading and talking, and just sitting in the sun as the weather got progressively hotter. The ship was not in convoy, but sailing alone with one destroyer escort. It went far out into the Atlantic, then turned east, and ten days later land was sighted and we entered harbour at Freetown in West Africa, where the heat was stifling. There were many other ships in the harbour. A destroyer released depth-charges outside the harbour, having presumably detected a submarine. Three days later, the ship put to sea again, and in another fortnight arrived in Durban, South Africa. We then went by train to the Imperial Forces Transhipment Camp at Clairwood, just outside Durban. South Africa was a new world to all of us, far removed from the austerity of England. There was no blackout, and the shops were full of things unobtainable at home. The first items I bought were a big slab of chocolate and a tin of sweetened condensed milk, both of which I consumed as soon as I got back to camp. I used to go to the cinema every day in Durban with Peter Taylor and Maurice Gregson, and often we went swimming. Only one other thing stands out in my mind about that time, which was an organised visit to the Lever Brothers soap factory.

After some ten days at Durban we were entrained for a two-day journey up through the Drakensberg mountains to the high veldt, to yet another holding unit at Nigel. This was an aerodrome, an Advanced Flying Training School, where pupil pilots trained on Oxfords. A week later postings came through and were dispersed to various Elementary Flying Training Schools to train on Tiger Moths. I came under the instruction of a South African officer, Lieutenant Goddard, not the easiest of men to get on with and somewhat anti-British. Circuits and landings was the first part of the programme, for which we flew about twenty miles to Rietgat, a small auxiliary aerodrome, just a part of the veldt fenced in by barbed wire. Apart from circuits, the flying was done from the main aerodrome at Kroonstad, Orange Free State. Eventually I had a solo test with Lieutenant Hooper, and did two solo circuits, going on later to solo steep turns, spins and loops. Three thousand feet was the statutory minimum for loops, but I always went up to four, being a great believer in plenty of height. They always say that the two most useless things in flying are height above you and runway behind you.

When I had done ten and a half hours solo, an incident occurred with Lieutenant Goddard that put paid to my aspirations of becoming a pilot. We flew to Rietgat and carried out various exercises, then Lieutenant Goddard said: 'Just do one solo circuit, Wagner, then we'll go back to Kroonstad. Don't take long over it because I'll have another pupil waiting.' He took out his control column, secured the straps, and off I went. As I said, it was a very small field, and as I came in over the wire I could see I was too high, so I opened and went round again. This time also I was still too high and opened up again. I saw Lieutenant Goddard standing on one corner of the field waving his control column in the air and obviously in a rage. The third time I was on the high side again, but I thought to myself that I had to get down at all costs. The Tiger Moth ran and ran – having no brakes I could not arrest its progress, and it stopped about two yards from the wire, too close to turn it under power. So I undid my straps, got out, caught it by the tail-skid, pulled it back a few yards, turned it, got back in, and taxied back to where Lieutenant Goddard was waiting. 'Right Wagner,' he said, 'fly me back to Kroonstad and make a good job of it because it is the last time you'll be at the controls.' And regretfully that was the end of my pilot training. I was 'washed out' as the saying went, and was, of course, very disappointed.

Within three days I was on my way to Roberts Heights, Pretoria, where I was regraded as a navigator. The three weeks I spent there were just time-wasting, doing odd jobs and often going into Pretoria to the cinema, waiting for a vacancy at a Navigational Training School. Eventually a posting came through to No. 43 Air School, East London, which was quite a long way off. The train journey was through some spectacular scenery, down through the mountains to the coast. This was an Initial Training School where the rudiments of navigation were taught. I was, in fact, starting again from scratch.

Here I met Graham Walker who had been at the University Air Squadron with me, and who had been graded as a navigator from the start, and we kept together. For the first three weeks nothing much happened, and Graham and I spent most of our time in town going to the cinema or swimming in the Indian Ocean from Orient Beach. We did quite a lot of PT, had a few rugby games, and participated in a lot of rifle and ordinary drills. While doing rifle drill one day the station warrant officer, Warrant Officer Barrett, came out to watch. He was a big, fat man with piggy little eyes, a most unpleasant character. Observing the manoeuvre 'put down arms', when the rifle had to be laid on the ground, he remarked: 'You bloody lot remind me of a lot of WAAFs getting down on a jerry', and I thought to myself, 'What a common man, what a low lad.' Eventually the course proper started, with lectures on DR navigation, plotting, meteorology, armament, signals, radio-navigation, aircraft recognition, compasses and astro-navigation. This was all very concentrated stuff and lasted for ten weeks, ending with an examination.

At the end of the course postings came through and I went with two friends, Graham Walker and Dave Wright, on an overnight train journey down the coast to Port Alfred, a small town miles from anywhere. This was where the practical navigation took place, interspersed with lectures. We were billeted in tents. There was a beautiful beach, almost deserted, where huge rollers came in from the Indian Ocean, picked you up and tumbled you along through the surf. There were sharks outside the line of breakers, so you had to be wary about going any further out.

The flying training was done in Ansons, with South African Air Force units. Their Ansons did not have hydraulics on the undercarriage, and it had to be wound up by hand, which was an awful chore. But it was all right letting it down, though. On alternate flights one was either first or second navigator. The first navigator was responsible for plotting, wind-finding, working out courses, ground speed and time of arrival, while the second navigator did photography and obtained fixes and bearings using the astro-compass. All very well in the clear daylight skies of South Africa, but not likely to be much use in Europe where the ground was mostly obscured by cloud and everything was blacked-out at night. Also, the second navigator took sights on stars, using a sextant, but astro-fixes were far from reliable. Sights had to be taken on two stars and the readings converted into position lines, using the Air Almanac publication. It took about twenty minutes to get a fix plotted, by which time you were about forty miles further on.

And so the course continued until the middle of December. There were written examination in all subjects. The last flight was a long navigational exercise, from the eastern side of the country to the western, and was by way of being a celebration. Base–Uitenhage–out to sea–George –Oudtshoorn–Youngsfield (just outside Capetown). We stayed two days in a hotel in Capetown, and were disappointed not to be able to go up

Table Mountain, as the weather closed in. We flew back to Port Alfred, and that was the end of the course.

On 23 December 1943 the passing out parade took place and brevets were pinned on with all due formality. Sergeant's stripes were sewn on later on to best blue, battledress and great coat. That evening there was a flight dinner at the Bothurst Hotel in Port Alfred. The traditional services Christmas dinner took place on the 25th, all serving being done by the officers.

We left Port Alfred on Boxing Day, for the two and a half day journey back to Clairwood Camp, Durban. There was the usual splitting up of friends on posting, but by this time I was in the company of Leslie Shawcross. Shawcross had crashed on a low-level map-reading exercise, when the pilot flew too low and the aircraft skated across the countryside, so he had had a narrow escape, very nearly being yet another of the many thousands killed in training.

And so we moved on into 1944. At Clairwood we were members of the Sergeants' Mess, and this was quite a luxurious place, with very good food and a bar. There was plenty of free time and no harassment, as we were just waiting for a ship back to England. We were not waiting long – on 6 January we embarked in Durban harbour on the SS *Arundel Castle*, a ship of 19,000 tons. We were on an upper deck this time, sleeping in bunks instead of hammocks. Unfortunately for me mine was the top of a stack of four, right under an emergency light that had to be left on all night and shone directly into my face. Furthermore, a card school gathered below and played all night, with frequent calls of 'Twist', 'Bust', 'I'll see you', so sleep was intermittent. Life aboard was generally very leisurely, though, with the occasional gun crew, lookout, or messing duties, and most of the time was spent reading, talking or seeing cinema shows.

On 7 January we were tugged out of Durban harbour, and steamed around waiting for the convoy to assemble. On 12 January we entered Mombasa harbour; little did I know I would be there again twenty-three years later. We left that same day, headed out to sea and then turned north. On 17 January we reached the harbour at Aden, left the next day and steamed into the Red Sea, and thence to the Gulf of Suez, where we anchored. Aircrew destined for the Middle East disembarked here, mostly South Africans.

Although the ship was anchored some two miles offshore, an all-pervading smell of burning tar and sulphur wafted out over us, it's purpose being, so we were told, to counteract an outbreak of bubonic plague onshore. The ship steadily filled up with naval and RAF personnel heading for home, and there was little room to move about. On 2 February we entered the Suez Canal. About halfway along the canal it passed through the wide expanse of the Bitter Lakes, and it was the practice for north- and south-bound convoys to pass each other at this point. There was a lot to be seen there – ex-Italian warships, submarines, flak ships, army camps, gun positions. All those aboard the troopship were able to indulge in the luxury of shouting abuse and obscenities at military police on guard at the gate of an army camp, about twenty yards away. The canal was very narrow, and there was only ten yards to spare on either side of the ship. At Port Said, after passage through the canal, we took on oil and water from tankers, joined a convoy of four other troopships and three destroyers, and moved out into the Mediterranean. Torches and emergency rations were issued, as the northern coasts of the Med were still in German hands and there was still enemy activity, although by this time the North African coast was in our hands. This coast was plainly visible to port, between Tobruk and Benghazi. Four days later the coast of Sicily was sighted. The rest of the convoy went off to Italy and the *Arundel Castle* and *Stirling Castle* entered harbour at Port Augusta. We left next day, joined a new convoy and headed west, the next stop being at Algiers for one day. This was the last stopover on the way home. We passed the lights of Tangier to port, sailed through the Straits of Gibraltar, round the north of Ireland and into the Mersey, where we disembarked immediately and proceeded by train to Harrogate. There was not much to be done there – kit inspections, medicals, documentation – and at the end of February I went home to Henley on leave for three weeks, returning to Harrogate thereafter.

After a few days at Harrogate a posting came through to Whitley Bay, Northumberland. This was yet another holding unit. Aircrew were churned out from the training schools then gradually moved up the line as vacancies occurred, heading inevitably for squadron status. There was always an ample pool of trained men to draw upon. In Whitley Bay we were billeted in ex-seaside boarding houses. I was not sorry to leave Whitley Bay.

The next posting was to an Advanced Flying Unit at West Freugh, near Stranraer in Scotland. There was, of course, more waiting about while things got organised – lectures on the Browning gun, firing it on the range, dinghy drill, hydraulic systems of aircraft, flying control, night vision, beacons and occults, radio procedures, astro, parachute drill and 'airmanship' (which covered just about everything). Here I made the acquaintance of 'Biff' Brewer, so called because he was a keen golfer. Fortunately, the sports officer was also a keen golfer and he often gathered together a few aficionados and took us to Portpatrick Golf Club where the professional had sets of clubs that he loaned out. It was a good course, along the clifftops, from where you could see Ireland across the water. There was a flying boat base at Stranraer and Sunderlands could be seen taking off and alighting in the loch.

At West Freugh we had individual photographs taken. These were intended to be handed to resistance groups in the event of being shot down, to aid in the preparation of false papers, and were known as 'pimpernel' photos.

Flying training was done on Ansons on this course, an extension of the work carried out in South Africa, but under more difficult conditions. The weather was much worse, and on night flying there were no lights to be seen, only the beacons and occults, and more use had to be made of radio bearings. The routes were generally north-west over the Irish Sea, where there would be less traffic, a typical one being Base–Ayr–Rathlin Island (Northern Ireland)–Dungannon–Peel (Isle of Man)–Base.

This course lasted six weeks or so, then the next posting was to an Operational Training Unit at Abingdon. There were talks on new aspects of navigation, such as navigating on the climb and descent, and on Gee, a radar device that enabled the navigator to secure an instant and very accurate fix – no more need for getting position lines and transferring them as necessary. There was much practice in plotting in the navigational trainer. There were also lectures on the German Air Force, and other intelligence matters, and on escaping and evasion.

At Abingdon crewing-up took place. Twenty pilots, twenty navigators, twenty bomb-aimers, twenty wireless operators and forty gunners were assembled in a hall and left to their own devices. It was up to each one to slot himself in, and in the end twenty crews emerged. My own crew consisted of pilot Wilfred Bates from Newcastle, myself as navigator, bomb aimer Leslie Roberts from Liverpool, wireless operator Jack Jones from Lampeter, mid-upper gunner Thomas Worthington from Liverpool, and rear gunner Robert Thomas from Whitehaven. There was no need for a flight engineer at this stage, as training was carried out on Armstrong Whitworth Whitleys, which only had two engines. Later, while at a Heavy Conversion Unit, we were joined by Eric Berry from Sale.

The Whitley was a heavy bomber in service at the beginning of the war, but since superseded. It was not a pleasant aircraft to fly in, being very cramped, cold, lumbering and having no radar navigational equipment. Also it was somewhat difficult to get out of in an emergency. The wing chord was very thick, the two wings being joined by a narrow tunnel across the fuselage, through which one had to crawl to reach the escape hatch, encumbered by heavy flying gear and a parachute pack. It was engined by two Rolls-Royce Merlins. The Whitleys we trained on were tired and worn out, and would not get above 12,000 feet.

As runways were being laid at Abingdon we moved to Stanton Harcourt, a satellite for Abingdon, and flew from there. The flights in the Whitley were longer than those in the Anson, a typical one being Stanton Harcourt–Newquay–Milford Haven–Stanton Harcourt, about four and a half hours, including an hour or so on the bombing range. One trip I have noted shows some of the difficulties that could be encountered: 'Took off in fine weather 10.30, but ran into cloud half-way to Newquay. Started to descend, but the cloud got lower and thicker. Climbed to 12,000 feet, but icing started so went down to 7,000 feet, still in cloud. Spotted a hole in the clouds, and went down through it to have a look. Identified position as Falmouth. Headed north, homed along the St Eval beam, landed, and had dinner. Took off again 15.00 and flew low along the coast, looking upwards at the cliffs off Hartland Point as we passed. Cut inland at Burnham and flew eastwards via Swindon through low cloud and bad weather, back to Stanton Harcourt.'

Apart from the long trips there were many shorter ones, such as practice on the bombing range and fighter affiliation, and quite a few navigational trips in Ansons while pilots were on familiarisation on the Whitleys.

The OTU course finished early in August; we returned to Abingdon and a couple of days later went on leave. After that ended the next posting was to No. 4 Group Aircrew Training School, Acaster Malbis, near York. Being now in No. 4 Group meant that we would be operating on Halifaxes. Training school it might have been, but it was in fact yet another holding unit. Nevertheless, there were lectures on many diverse topics such as broadcast wind velocities for bombing, pathfinder techniques, pyrotechnics, oscilloscopes, dinghy radios, hydraulic systems, German targets, flak, H2S, air position indicator, homing on Gee, airborne lifeboat – all good stuff.

The next move was to No. 1652 Heavy Conversion Unit, Marston Moor, near York. Here we were introduced to the Handley Page Halifax Mark III, on which we would be operating. Pilots had to learn the technique of flying a large four-engined aircraft, and the rest of the crew had to familiarise themselves with their position in the plane and new equipment, as well as the general layout of the aircraft, such as flare-chutes, escape hatches, oxygen equipment etc. The Halifax was engined with four Bristol Hercules sleeve-valve engines, and its all-up weight was some 30 tons. It did not quite match up to the Lancaster in performance and weight-lifting, but it was a good airman's aircraft, solid, robust and very dependable – it could take more knocking about than a Lancaster. It cruised at about 230 knots indicated airspeed when light, 210 when loaded. Fuel consumption was 0.9 air miles per gallon, and it could carry about 5 tons of bombs, depending on the distance of the target. The bomb load was usually mixed – perhaps one 2,000-pounder, two 1,000-pounders, four 500-pounders and the rest made up of incendiaries, either 30-pounders or canisters of 4-pounders. The aim was to knock the target about and then set fire to it.

At Marston Moor we were joined by flight engineer Eric Berry and were now a complete crew of seven.

The first few Halifax flights were for Wilfred Bates to learn how to handle the Halifax and get used to doing so, including three-engined flying, and for the bomb aimer to drop practice bombs on the range, so there was not much for me to do – just keep tabs on where we were. Even if lost it was easy enough to get a Gee fix and give a course for base. Air-to-air firing, for the benefit of the gunners, took place out at sea, beyond Flamborough Head. Flying was often cancelled through bad weather, or because of unserviceability of aircraft, since these were rather tired ex-operational aeroplanes, or ones that had been damaged in accidents. After about a fortnight of this sort of thing the time came to venture further afield. The first attempt was a failure – Base climbing to 16,000 feet – March – then the port inner engine packed up, so the propeller was feathered and we returned to base. It was another fortnight before we did a navigational trip again, the only flying in the meantime being night circuits. Much of the time in between was spent going into York to the pictures with one or more of the crew, or drinking in the Boot and Shoe or Spotted Ox at Tockwith, the nearest village.

A typical cross-country was Base–Darlington–Goole–Bury St Edmunds –Market Harborough–Coventry–Nottingham–Base, but equipment of some sort often misbehaved – such as one of the engines, Gee, H2S or DR compass – involving an early return. Sometimes we did not even get off the ground, as equipment proved unserviceable on being tested, or flying was cancelled at the last moment. If anything went wrong with the flying of the aircraft, there was a very efficient service known as Darkie. The procedure was to call Darkie and on enquiring the nature of the emergency, type of aircraft, whether heavy or light (i.e. bombs onboard or not), they would give a course to fly to the nearest aerodrome that could accept the aircraft and monitor your progress to it. One such occasion I recorded reads: 'After 20 minutes port inner packed up. Called Darkie and landed at 2125 at Bottesford, near Nottingham, a Lancaster Conversion Unit. Reported in at Flying Control, drew blankets, had supper, and turned in. Left 1430 the next day and flew back to base.'

At the end of the Heavy Conversion Unit course, the sausage machine churned out the next and final posting, which was to No. 51 Squadron at Snaith, not far from Doncaster. We were now a fully trained crew ready to be let loose on the Germans. All the crew members were billeted together in a Nissen hut, which was shared with one other crew. Most of the day-time was spent in the Navigation Section or in the Bombing Section with Robbie, doing nothing in particular, playing draughts perhaps or Chinese checkers. The radio was always playing, a popular tune at that time being, 'Would you like to swing on a star/Carry moonbeams home in a jar …'. I became heartily sick of that tune and still dislike it even now. Other tunes that were all the rage were, 'I hate to see that evening sun go down' (true enough) and, prophetically, 'Don't fence me in'.

The first few flights were familiarisation of various sorts – practice bombing, air-to-air firing, fighter affiliation. On the first flight we did three circuits, then a tyre burst, so that was the end of that. On the first cross-country, which was up to Scotland, down to the Isle of Man and back to base, bad weather prevented us landing there and we were diverted to Melbourne, returning to Snaith the next day. The next cross-country was Base–York–Belfast–Liverpool–Sheffield–Base, and was for practice in using the navigational aid H2S. On a Halifax there was a bulge under the fuselage towards the tail. This contained a rotating scanner. When radio waves were transmitted from it and hit something vertical they were reflected back and showed as white patches on the appropriate receiver at the navigator's position. Thus towns displayed extremely well and could be identified from a special map. Open ground presented quite clearly too; from water there was no return. Controls on the set enabled the navigator to get his bearing and distance once the pinpoint was identified.

On 16 November we were awoken at 07.40 hours by an airman, and navigators were told to report to the Navigation Department for preliminary briefing for operations. This was so that navigators would know the target in advance (being warned to keep their mouths shut about it), and be able to get part of their work done beforehand. This consisted of marking turning points, drawing in tracks on the charts, measuring the compass bearing of each and the distance, and seeing that everyone was in agreement. Then we had breakfast at 09.20 and went to the Briefing Room at 10.00, with complete crews, for the main briefing, attended by the commanding officer, Wing Commander Holford, navigation officer, bombing leader, met. officer, intelligence officer and armament officer. Afterwards everyone repaired to the locker room and put on flying gear, flying boots lined with lambswool, and parachute harness. Contents of pockets were handed in, helmet, goggles and oxygen mask picked up, as well as three pairs of gloves (woollen, silk and leather gauntlets), microphone and intercom lead. I carried the gloves only for use in emergency, in case of fire, and goggles for the same reason. If so desired one could draw a revolver and six rounds, which I always did. You never knew when it might be needed; one of the great fears was coming down in the target area, where the natives would be vicious, and five rounds could be used on the Germans, the last one being kept for personal use.

So with all this gear, parachute pack and navigation log containing all the necessary equipment (pencils, rubber, ruler, charts, Douglas protractor, dividers, Dalton computer) I repaired to the aircraft together with the rest of the crew. We took off at 12.50 hours and did a 'radius of action'. This was necessary so that the whole squadron could set course over base at the same time. In order not to have a lot of aircraft milling about in the circuit at the same time, each navigator was given a track outward from base, towards the north-west, each a few degrees different from one another so that aircraft coming back did not collide with any still outward bound. It was up to each navigator to determine his course to fly to maintain that track, and how long to fly it before turning to arrive over base at the appointed time of departure. In this case it was 13.40, and the target was Jülich, a small town not far from Aachen, only just inside Germany, being used as a supply and transit centre for the front-line forces, so we were not long over hostile territory. Bombing height was low, 10,000 feet. There was a little flak and no fighters. At the same time a force of Lancasters were attacking Duren, a similar town a few miles to the south. It was an uneventful trip, but very effective, as reported in the next day's *Daily Telegraph*:

> **Two Rhine Towns Written Off**
> *Photographs of Duren and Julich taken two days after they were attacked by very large forces of RAF bombers on November 16 show a close concentration of bomb craters almost without parallel in any previous attacks by the RAF. The centres of both were recently fortified towns, which were among the main defences of the Rhine, have been completely destroyed.*

The following day, bombing photographs were on the board in the Intelligence Room. A camera was always operated a certain number of seconds after the bomb release was pressed and took a photo of the point of the impact. Our photo was in the centre, and enlarged, and showed the best strikes of the squadron, 200 yards from the centre of the town.

The second operation took place on 18 November and was another daylight trip. The target was Münster. Navigators' briefing was before breakfast, the main briefing after. We took off at 12.45 hours, performing a radius of action, and then set course at 13.25. Flak was light and no fighters were seen. Münster was covered by cloud. Concentration appeared poor on this attack. A word here about target marking. There were two methods, 'Newhaven' and 'Wanganui'. Newhaven was used when the target was clear of cloud. Pathfinder 'illuminators' would go in first and drop white flares, by whose light the second lot of Pathfinders could identify the aiming point. As near to this as possible they dropped the appropriate marker flares. There were several different sorts – red shooting yellow stars, green shooting red stars etc. – and bomb aimers knew which to look for. This did not give the Germans time to confuse the issue with their own flares some distance away. Most large German targets had decoy sites a few miles away where fires were often lit to simulate an attack, and these did at times attract a number of bombs. Wanganui marking was used when the target was obscured. Pathfinders dropped parachute flares upwind of the aiming point, or rather upwind of the centre of the town. These burned for two minutes or so and bomb aimers trained on them. This method was obviously not so precise as Newhaven, but it ensured a good spread of bombs, hopefully in the target area. Flares had to be continuously renewed throughout the attack. Always some Pathfinders were Wanganui-equipped just in case the target could not be seen. So after briefing the instruction was, 'Newhaven with emergency Wanganui.'

If all else failed, and nothing could be seen, bombs could be dropped by making use of the navigational device Gee. This was accurate to within a quarter of a mile or so, and was therefore acceptable for this purpose. The bombsight was not used, and bombs were released on instructions from the navigator. Gee, however, could not be employed on distant targets. It depended on signals sent out from England and was susceptible to jamming. As one proceeded further away from the transmitting station the signals became weaker and more difficult to identify, and on the cathode-ray tube gradually disappeared among all the clutter provided by the Germans. On some raids a master bomber would orbit higher up, watching progress and giving instructions. There was a natural tendency for bomb aimers to release the load a few seconds early, and this progression led to a 'creep back', so that the master bomber had to advise a change of aiming point. I heard once a directive from him: 'Apple Pie to main force. Bomb upwind edge of smoke.' And this later, when we were on our way home, 'Well done chaps. Now get off home and have your breakfast.'

On return from the Münster attack, Warrant Officer Bruce crashed in a collision while waiting to land. After putting all the gear away crews were debriefed by specialist officers who took notes on how things had gone and anything unusual that might have happened, and while this was going on mugs of thick cocoa were provided and tots of rum. I always took the rum neat but there were some who tipped it into their cocoa, and almost unbelievably some who refused it altogether. After the second operation we went on leave for ten days, during which Bob Thomas, our rear gunner, got married.

Two days after our return, operations were notified, the target being Essen in the Ruhr. Navigators' briefing took place at 8pm, main briefing at 11. Take-off time was 02.26 hours, with a radius of action and set course at 03.11. Usual route was base–Reading–Beachy Head–over to France. We arrived over the target just two minutes later and bombed using Wanganui flares at 05.39, before arriving back at base at 08.23 hours. Breakfast followed a debriefing before falling into bed and sleeping until 5 o'clock.

There had been heavy flak during the operation, with some fighters in the target area, and this would be a suitable juncture to digress for a few words on flak. Intelligence knew where the heaviest concentrations of flak were, and aircraft were routed to avoid them, but there was no dodging it on the approach to and over the target. Bombing heights usually varied from 21,000 to 18,000 feet, different waves of aircraft being allocated different heights. The Germans, knowing this, could only spread their shells about, barrage fashion, filling the sky with as many explosives as possible, in the hope of catching something random. The greatest concentrations were naturally north, west and south of the target, and it was not possible to avoid them. You could not go over the top because the aircraft, loaded, would not go high enough. You could not go round the outside because fighters lurked there and anyway everybody would be coming in at different angles, causing collisions galore. You could not go underneath because of the risk of 'friendly' bombs falling on you. So the only thing you could do was get your head down and run the gauntet hell for leather through the middle, hoping that nothing had got your name on it. I only looked out twice over the target; it was like a fairground on a Saturday night – target indicators, fires burning, photo flashes going off, anti-aircraft shells bursting, searchlights. After that I just didn't want to know, preferring the scholarly calm of the 'office'.

The following night there was an operation on Duisburg (docks and transport). It was an uneventful trip. Took off at 16.40 hours, radius of action, set course 17.14. Base–Reading–Beachy Head–France–Duisburg. Surprisingly, flak was negligible, with no fighters. Bombed at 20.06 on Wanganui flares, and arrived back at base at 23.40, followed by supper and into bed by 01.00.

The next operation was two nights later, on Hagen in the Ruhr. Set course 18.14. Over Reading the port inner engine failed so we went north-east and jettisoned the bombs in the North Sea beyond Flamborough Head, and returned to base.

On Monday 4 December there was a short local trip, down to Derby, followed by a blind bombing run on York, using H2S. A further word about H2S here. It was quite accurate on a fairly large target (provided it had been positively identified first – not much use, though, in a large conurbation such as the Ruhr). The bombs were released on instructions from the navigator. I did not like using H2S for any purpose, and steered clear of it except in the case of necessity. German fighters were known to home on to its transmissions, so I left it switched off as far as possible.

At this moment it would be fitting to describe briefly the modus operandi of the German night-fighter force. The ever increasing activities of Bomber Command forced the Germans to withdraw large numbers of fighters from other fronts, so there were plenty of them about, mostly in Holland, northern France and western Germany. The single-engined types were Me109s and FW190s; the twin-engined were Me110s, Me210s, a small number of the later Me410s, and, most effective of all, Ju88s, which started out early in the war as bombers but were later converted largely to night fighting. The single-engined aircraft operated on a system that the Germans called 'Wild Boar'. They were vectored on to the bomber stream and left to their own devices to find and attack as best they could. The twin-engined planes functioned on the 'Tame Boar' system, and came under close control from the ground. They were also equipped with radar, so that once they latched on to a target they were hard to shake off. The two standard methods of evasion were a violent 'corkscrew' motion or a fierce diving turn to port or starboard. Knowing that its presence had been detected a fighter would often go and try its luck elsewhere, hoping for a more unwary victim.

There was a device called Mandrel. Aircraft of No. 100 Group (countermeasures), usually Stirlings (which were not fit for bomber operations because they could not operate at a high level), flew a 'race course' pattern out in the Channel, jamming the German Wurzburgs, which were long-range detectors. The Germans therefore knew that a raid was pending, but did not know where the main force would emerge from behind the screen. So they had two radio beacons a long way from each other, called Otto and Ida, and fighters orbited these beacons waiting for the main force to manifest itself, and when it did, half of them anyway were in the vicinity. It became the practice for the RAF to insert a Mosquito bomber among those orbiting these beacons and the crew might be lucky enough to shoot down a couple of the enemy before they rumbled what was going on and dispersed. At any rate, it made the Germans nervous and threw them out of gear. This operation was known as a 'Mahmoud'. There were many other operations designed to deceive and disrupt. A Mosquito would lurk near every enemy fighter aerodrome and catch fighters taking off or returning to refuel. 'Spoof' raids would take place by smaller forces on widely separated targets, or just several aircraft dropping target indicators and then nothing else happening.

In the second half of 1944 the Germans hit upon the most effective way of dealing with a bomber once it was found and identified; so simple that it is amazing it was never thought of before, and it was a long time before anyone twigged what was happening. Early in the war some aircraft, notably Wellingtons, had a turret underneath, but the fitting of these was discontinued, so there was no protection from below. Two tail warning and downward-looking radars, Monica and Fishpond, were fitted, but these were removed when it was found that the Germans were homing on to them. Realising they had a clear field from underneath, a German fighter, invisible against the dark background below, would gradually increase its height until it was some 150 to 200 feet below the bomber, with the bomber silhouetted against the lighter sky above and its exhaust flames clearly visible. On the same course and at the same speed the bomber was a sitting duck. German twin-engined fighters had a cannon sticking out through the roof, known as 'schräge musik', and the gunner could let rip with a no-deflection shot. They always aimed for the starboard wing tanks, not the fuselage where there would be a risk of detonating explosives on board. Having thus set the aircraft on fire the enemy departed in search of other prey. They carried no tracer among their ammunition, so that there was no give-away, and a bomber seemed to others around just to catch fire for no apparent reason.

To return to events at Snaith, on Tuesday 5 December the warning was given at 11.30 hours for operations that night, the target being Soest on the eastern edge of the Ruhr, which meant flying all the way round that industrial and heavily defended complex. Main briefing was at 14.15, then out to the aircraft before returning for alterations to the flight plan. Take-off was at 17.00 and set course at 18.00. We arrived over the target two minutes late and bombed on Gee, as the bombsight was unserviceable. Flak was heavy over Hamm on the way but was light over the target. After a nine-hour trip, we returned to base at 02.00. Four aircraft went missing on this attack.

The following night operations were laid on against Osnabrück, taking off at 16.00 hours, with a set course at 16.25. Down to Reading at 2,000 feet, and saw Henley on the port side on the way. Passed over Reading Bridge when workers were on their journeys home and the lights of vehicles were clearly visible. The sky was full of aircraft heading south-east. Climbed through icing cloud, proceeded on time over France and so to the target, one of the first aircraft in. Bombed on Gee. Then it was out in a northerly direction over Holland, arriving back at base at 22.10, a six-hour trip. Flak had been very heavy over the target. Eight aircraft were missing after this attack.

The next day we did dinghy drill in a reservoir, very cold, wet and muddy. On the 9th we did a practice flight, three simulated bombing runs on York, followed by practice bombs on the range. On the 10th we were roused at 02.45 for operations, but cancellation came through after the main briefing, the target having been Bielefeld (presumably the viaduct). This was laid on again the next day, but scratched again when everybody had got their flying kit on. On the 12th an operation was laid on against Essen: flight planning 12.00, main briefing 13.30, took off 16.00, set course 16.20, bombed on Wanganui flares 19.39, and arrived back at base 22.00. There had been heavy flak in the target area, as was to be expected over the Ruhr. Six aircraft failed to return. On the 15th an operation was laid on against Dortmund but later abandoned.

On the evening of 17 December a briefing took place for an attack on Duisburg at 22.30 hours, then we had supper. We took off at 03.00 on the usual route via Reading and Beachy Head, and out over France. The weather deteriorated rapidly, wind velocity rose to over 100 knots, and the meteorological forecast was all wrong, so that the main force became widely scattered. Although we tried to make up a bit of time by cutting corners, nevertheless we arrived over the target seven minutes late. No marker flares were seen – with that wind velocity they would not have been much use, so we bombed using Gee. Soon after turning for home we were set upon by a twin-engined fighter, which was driven off three times by our gunners. There followed a short interval when he seemed to have gone elsewhere, but such was not the case.

Here, I will digress and consider the possibility of surviving a tour of operations. I have already indicated that they were not very great. A tour consisted of thirty operations; average losses were about 4%, therefore after twenty-five trips a man was statistically dead, and therefore again the average man could expect to last twelve or thirteen sorties. Some of course were unlucky on their first and some on their thirtieth, and obviously you needed a lot of good fortune on your side – it was not just a matter of skill. A flak shell could catch any crew, no matter how experienced. As to the attitude of aircrew in general, there was a certain amount of fatalism involved, induced by the perithanatic situation in which they found themselves. The Greek word 'Peri' means 'around' and 'thanatos' means 'death', and psychologists say that when in this situation there is an acceptance of what is going to happen and it ceases to worry. Personally, I never saw in others any evidence of fear – apprehension, yes, but not fear. When I say that the average man could expect to last twelve or thirteen trips (i.e. rather less than half a tour), this is borne out by the overall statistics of Bomber Command for the whole of the war – some 125,000 men flew with Bomber Command and 55,573 were killed. As I write this it is Remembrance Sunday and I am reminded of a remark by Richard Dimbleby commenting on one of these services at the Cenotaph: 'Those that took the wings of the morning, or set their course by the stars into unimaginable dangers. . . .' The hazards were well enough known, though, 'and their name was legion, for they were many'. – flak, fighters, mechanical malfunction, icing, cumulo-nimbus clouds and lightning, base fogged in on return, shortage of petrol, collision, fire, to name but a few. In church the preacher, Canon Hartley, an ex-prisoner of the Japanese, said, 'I wonder how long Remembrance Day will go on. Until, I suppose, there is nobody left who remembers.'

To return to the situation in which we found ourselves, after three or four minutes, there was a series of thumps from the starboard wing, and almost immediately the flight engineer said 'Wilf, we're on fire.' I looked back from my position down in the nose, and could see that there was a roaring mass of flames where the wing root joined the fuselage and that the situation was obviously beyond control – burning petrol was swilling in from the tanks, round the oxygen bottles, which would explode in due course. There was only one thing to do, which was to get out, and that right speedily, because one of two things was going to happen in a very short time. Either the tanks would explode or the main spar would melt and the wing would fall off. So even before the order came to abandon the aircraft I was already buckling my parachute pack on to the harness. My seat, on springs, folded itself against the starboard wall when I stood up. I kicked away the legs of the navigator's table, which folded itself down on to the port wall, leaving an open space on the floor with the escape hatch in the middle. This was the way out for the three of us in the nose – myself, bomb aimer and radio operator. The mid-upper gunner would use the entrance door halfway back down the fuselage, but the turret was difficult to get out of, and it took time. The rear gunner would swivel his turret and drop out over the end, but again the turret was not easy to remove oneself from and furthermore his parachute pack was stored in the fuselage outside the turret. The pilot and flight engineer would use whichever exit they could get at most quickly. I opened the hatch, raised it above the vertical, lifted it off its hinges, and shoved it through the hole. I then sat on the forward edge of the hatch and dropped out into the night sky.

A few words of explanation is needed about how the parachute harness was designed. The pack was clipped on to two buckles on separate straps that came down from the shoulders and were attached to the main harness straps by two pieces of string. The intention was that when the parachute opened the string would snap, the pack would swing upwards, and you were left suspended from the shoulders. As I plunged through the hole, though, the pack caught on the rear edge, snapping the string, so that by the time I was in free fall, the pack was way up above my head, and to make matters worse the release ring was facing backwards, so that I had to haul it down and scrabble about to find the release ring behind the back of my head. It was a relief therefore when there was a violent jerk as the parachute opened and I was safely on the way down. The aircraft had been at a height of 14,000 feet, and the descent would take about a quarter of an hour. After a few seconds there was a 'whoomph' as the tanks blew up and I did not know whether anybody else had got clear. There were flashes of light and a rumbling in the distance, which I took to be thunder, but realised later was anti-aircraft fire; also, it was raining hard.

As a factual observation, and with no intent to blow my own trumpet, there was no feeling of fear or panic in me – fear only comes when one has an alternative and in this case there was not one; there was only one thing I was able to do – float earthwards – and it produced rather a feeling of annoyance that when I got down I was going to be caught and stuck inside for the rest of the war. One of the advantages of being the navigator was that I had a pretty good idea of where we were. I knew we were over the British side of the lines, but knew also that there was a strong westerly wind which would probably carry me back inside Germany. If you took an average wind speed on the way down of 80mph, I was going to drift some twenty miles. It was about 6.30am and still dark. Perhaps just a hint of daylight – 'dawn's left hand was in the sky' (Omar Khayyam) – so I could not see where I was going to land, and in fact lurched down through the branches of a tree before hitting the ground. The advice was that when you landed you were supposed to roll your parachute up and hide it. I realised this was not possible as it was draped over the tree. Furthermore it was an apple tree in the back garden of a house, and the curtains in one of the bedroom windows parted and a face peered out. So I took off my life jacket, dumped it, and went down the side path and out of the front gate. Turning left I heard the sound of marching feet approaching, so I turned promptly right, and in a few minutes was out of the village and in open country.

Chapter Fourteen

Hande Hoch

It was now getting light, and the thing to do was to find concealment wherein to lie up for the day. Soon I found a wood of fir trees and took refuge. First, judging by the sound of gunfire from the west, I knew I was in fact inside Germany. Then I examined the contents of my evasion pack. There was a flattish plastic box, slightly curved to fit inside the thigh pocket of a flying suit. It contained a map on silk, razor, rubber water bottle with a packet of Halazone water purifying tablets, energy tablets, Horlicks tablets, barley sugar and chewing gum, also a small compass about one-inch in diameter. And there was a small slab of nut toffee.

By this time my clothes were wet through, and it was cold as well, so I did not have a comfortable day. I set off walking south as soon as it was dark, keeping clear of the roads and going across country, over ditches full of water and through fences. The intention was to walk into France where I might make contact with the Resistance, and knowing the language would be a help. At daybreak heavy rain came down again. I hid in a small fir plantation after taking off my wet flying suit and boots, but could not sleep due to the cold and general discomfort. Some children with their mother and a couple of dogs passed within a few yards of me, but apparently didn't see me. I ate three Horlicks tablets, one chunk of toffee and a piece of barley sugar, which I planned to be my ration for two weeks. It was a bad time of the year for evasion, there being nothing in the fields in the way of berries, fruit or vegetables. I drank from streams or troughs, using the plastic water bottle and purifying tablets.

I set off again at dusk and walked until about 4am when I came across a barn and stepped inside. As soon as it was properly light I saw that there was a loft full of hay, with a ladder leading up to it. I climbed it, took off my wet flying suit and boots, stuffed them with hay, burrowed well down, and went to sleep. Not that stuffing them with hay did any good – they were still wet and cold when I put them on later. I pushed on again when it was dark, over the waterlogged fields. At daybreak I saw what appeared to be a dilapidated farmhouse, and I approached it with the intention of sleeping therein. It was occupied, though. A middle-aged woman came out, and must have recognised me for what I was. But she was not in any position to cause trouble, so I followed her inside and made sure there was nobody else in residence. She indicated that I was to sit at the table and gave me a few small apples, two slices of bread and two cups of coffee. It was, by now, broad daylight, so after leaving there was not time to look for a good place of concealment. The best I could do was a copse with wet brambles in it, so I hid up there for the day even though it was only half a mile or so from the farmhouse and one could expect that the German woman had gone to alert the authorities.

There was not much sleep that day because I kept waking up with severe cramp, induced no doubt by wearing wet clothes for too long. I decided it was no use going south, the distance being too great, so I turned back north towards Holland. There was no way of getting through the lines by going due west, and anyway that River Rhine was in the way, and that would be well guarded. However, the British advance northwards into Holland had been very rapid, and looked like continuing, so I thought I would head north-west round the corner in the lines and either hide up or maybe fall in with the Dutch Resistance until the fighting moved on further north. It was an outside chance, but any chance was better than none.

That night, 21 December, it rained hard again. Towards dawn I wandered about looking for somewhere dry to sleep. I stayed for a while in a shed beside the road, then it stopped raining so I carried on for another three miles. I found a stack of loose straw, so I dug some out, made a cubby hole in the side, climbed in, and went to sleep for the day.

I got out at dark, put on the flying suit, and set out again. That night it froze, and my flying suit, being wet, froze stiff and the zips would not work so I could not get out my ration pack. And I suffered pains from cramp again. I walked all night, breaking ice on puddles to drink from. By this time, for various reasons all added together, I was getting light in the head and not thinking very clearly. I came to a railway embankment and climbed up. When I got on to the track I thought, 'This is stupid. All I have to do is walk along until I come to a station and get a train home.' So I turned left and paced along the track for about twenty minutes. Seeing the lights of a station ahead, and hearing voices, brought me to my senses, so I hastily got down off the track and pushed on.

At daylight, bedded down in a partly cut wood of fir trees, American bombers passed overhead. I pressed on again at night, and without thinking what I was doing I went through a village instead of skirting around it as usual. At the far end there was the click of a rifle bolt and a voice, 'Halt. Wer da?' I knew that was the end of my run. 'Englische flieger,' I said, and the reply came, 'Hande hoch.' I had run into a sentry post. The soldier approached and indicated with his rifle that I should go into the post, which was a dugout about ten feet square, entered by going down some steps. In it there was a table, a chair and a bench, and it was heated by a wood burning stove and lit by a pressure lamp. The sentry was an oldish chap, well meaning and obviously not one to make life difficult. He didn't want any trouble, and I was in no state to give him any anyway. I patted the chest of my flying suit and said, 'Ich habe hier eine kanone', and he motioned I should put it on the table, meanwhile keeping me closely covered with his rifle. He indicated also that anything else in my pockets should be put on the table. After that the atmosphere became less strained and he provided me with a bowl of soup. Then, seeing my clothes were wet he told me to take them off and he hung them in front of the stove to dry, giving me his blanket to wrap round myself, and directing me to lie down on the bench and go to sleep. In the morning he permitted me to shave using the razor from my evasion pack and then gave me a slice of bread and some of his meat paste. As I said, not a bad old chap at all. By this time his relief had arrived and, being appraised of the state of affairs, went to fetch another man. With this new man and the old original guard I walked about eight kilometres to a fighter aerodrome at Alpen. This was on Christmas Eve.

I was taken into the Officers' Mess and subjected to all sorts of questions, but not of an operational nature, by those gathered therein.

None as it happened could speak English, but one spoke French, and he translated for the rest. He asked how many times I had been over Germany, and when I said 'eight' he said that was nothing, he had been over London sixty-six times. They were interested in my flying gear and also in the contents of my evasion pack. They gave me some of their dinner, which was a sort of spaghetti bolognaise, but I was shunted aside into an alcove to eat it on my own. I was then handed over to their service police and made to sit on a stool in the middle of the room, watched over by a surly individual with a rifle. After several hours of this my back ached, so I moved the stool against the wall, but an outburst and rifle waving indicated I should stay where I was put. That night I slept down in a warm cellar, locked in.

The next morning, Christmas Day, I left Alpen with one guard. We walked five kilometres then got a lift in a car to the nearest station and went by electric train to Düsseldorf. This was one of the RAF's main targets and was much knocked about. On the platform I noticed a rat-faced little man going from person to person, talking to them and pointing at me with a nod of the head. A few started drifting in my direction, and I didn't like the look of things at all, but the guard saw what was happening as well and unshouldered his rifle, which caused them to lose interest. Bomber crew were known throughout Germany as Terror-fliegers (terror flyers), which I used to think was unfair as we were only going about our lawful business, and I don't suppose German airmen considered themselves as Terrorfliegers when they were bombing English towns. On the other hand one can understand the attitude of civilians. The carpet bombing of German towns was aimed at breaking the will of the nation as a whole to continue the war, by means of fear and destruction. Any factories, military installations or transport facilities were a bonus unless they had been specially pinpointed for attack.

We stayed for an hour in the waiting room, then boarded a train to Frankfurt am Main, via Hagen and Giessen, which had at one time been subject to attack as the sidings were littered with smashed goods wagons. It had started to snow by this time and was bitterly cold in the train. Civilians sitting opposite were much interested in the nature and quality of my flying gear, especially the boots. On detraining at Frankfurt we walked a few kilometres to the aircrew interrogation centre at

Oberursel and I was handed in to official custody. My flying gear was all taken away, except for the boots, and I was shoved into a cell in solitary confinement. The cell measured about eight feet by four. There was a bench along one wall with a blanket, a small barred window high up and a light that never went out. There was a radiator below the window that came on at times during the day, but was off at night so that it was hard to sleep because of the cold, and to make matters worse footwear was taken away at night. There was a spyhole in the door, and beside the door a handle. To go to the toilet one pulled this handle, which caused a signal arm to clang down in the corridor outside. This brought along a guard who escorted one back and forth. Outside each cell was a box containing sheets of toilet paper. The first time I took two sheets, but it was made very plain to me that the standard ration was just one. Hard luck on anyone who happened to be suffering from a common prisoner of war complaint known as the squitters or screamers. The daily allowance of food was four slices of bread, one plate of soup and two cups of warm weak coffee without sugar or milk. I presume the object of this solitary confinement, without seeing anyone else and with absolutely nothing to do, was a sort of weakening up process, to make one more willing to talk when the time came for interrogation. It didn't bother me a lot, though as I have always been somewhat solitary by nature.

After two days I was taken out in the evening and up to a comfortably furnished softly lit room, smelling richly of cigar smoke, where an officer started off with general small talk and then came to air force matters. The Geneva Convention stated that all a prisoner was obliged to do is give his number, rank and name, which I did. He asked how long it was since I was shot down, and I saw no harm in answering that correctly, but when he said, 'That would be on the night of an attack on Duisburg' I thought I had said quite enough. When he asked about squadron number and type of aircraft I said, 'You know I can't give details such as that sir.' He persisted for a while with other questions, then gave up, and I was taken back to the cell for another couple of days, returning to the same room and interrogating officer as before. This time the approach was somewhat different. He began by remarking on the fact that I wore no identification discs. There were two of these, one round red one and one oblong green one with the corners chipped off. They were made of some sort of fibre, and the red one was fireproof. They were normally worn round the neck, but the string on mine had broken the day before the last flight and I was intending to renew it when I got back. The dialogue went something like this.

'There are two things that worry me about you Sergeant Wagner. Here we have one single man in RAF uniform who cannot, or will not, identify himself, and moreover claims a German name. How do I know you are who you say you are? Some details of your last flight might help to clear things up.'

I could see what he was getting at – a veiled threat – but I explained the matter of the identity discs, and said I could say no more. He continued.

'The second thing is that here we have an airman who has been wandering about in Germany for six days, claiming to have been shot down, but we have no others of the crew, and to crown it all, no wreckage of an aircraft that he came from. How do you explain this?'

'I jumped out over Holland and drifted back into Germany on the way down. Presumably the aircraft disintegrated over British-held territory.'

'Well, as it happens, Sergeant Wagner, I know more about you than you think. You are from 51 Squadron, Snaith, flying Halifaxes. The commanding officer is Wing Commander Holford, and …'

He went on to name the navigation leader, bombing leader and signals officer.

'You see, I have other crew from 51 Squadron, and they have said more than you are saying. Now, what I would like to know are what operations you have been on and what was your route and height to Duisburg, and what was the bomb load?'

'The bombload was no concern of mine. I don't know what it was. The height varied continually and I can't remember the exact routeing. Even if I could, the Geneva Convention only permits me to give number, rank and name.'

At this stage he desisted and I was returned to my cell. I was roused at 2am and given a piece of bread and a cup of coffee. Departing at 4am I walked with about fifty others, mostly Americans, to the station. We waited for about two hours in the cold and then went by train to Wetzlar, not a long journey, about two hours. We were marched four kilometres to a camp, searched again, given a POW capture parcel, and allocated a billet in a room of three-tier bunks containing some twenty men. The capture parcel was a small fibre suitcase containing pyjamas, towel, socks, shaving kit, soap, darning-holdall, toothbrush and toothpaste, comb, chocolate, and pipe and tobacco or cigarettes, and came by courtesy of the Red Cross. I dumped this on my bunk, stood up, and recognised the man in the bunk above. This was John Trumble, whom I had done some of my training with in South Africa, and we remained together through the hard times that lay ahead. His face lit up, and he exclaimed 'Waggie!' and I said, 'Hello John. A right old turn-up this, isn't it?' He had no other members of his crew with him either, so we teamed up. We spent six days altogether at Wetzlar – which was what would be called, I suppose, an aircrew disposal centre – always cold and hungry, and that took us over into January 1945.

There follow now some extracts from a diary I kept at the time, with some notes in brackets where further explanation is necessary.

5 January 1945
Posting lists up in the mess hall. I am going tomorrow with John to Stalag Luft 7, Bankau, Silesia.

6 January
Marched down to station in the afternoon, after being searched and given a packet of chewing gum each. Entrained in two cattle trucks, 25 to a truck. One Red Cross parcel between two issued for journey. Half the truck occupied by guards.

7, 8, 9 January
On the train.

10 January
Detrained 0800 and walked up to the camp through deep snow.
No greatcoats. Searched. Got a billet with John and we got organised in a combine with two others for food parcels and meals. Filled a paillasse with wood shavings.

11 January
One Red Cross parcel per man for fortnight promised and reasonable

German rations. First parcel 0815 and the other at 1615. Quite a good library. Snow on the ground all the time, and very cold. Got a greatcoat. Walked round perimeter track occasionally.

14 January
Went to church services in the evening. [The camp padre was an Army officer, Captain Collins. Air force padres were, in the nature of things, unlikely to be captured. Captain Collins was a remarkable man, but more of him later. A very large proportion of prisoners attended church services, not I think because there was nothing else to do but because a belief gave a man something to hold on to in difficult times.]

One evening there was a Russian air raid in the vicinity of the camp. I had just put margarine and honey on a slice of bread when the sirens went and the lights were turned out. So I put it down on a stool and went to look out of the window. When the lights came on again, no bread. Accusations of theft, but everybody denied responsibility. Then I saw a mangled piece of bread stuck to the seat of another man's trousers. I scraped it off and ate it.

18 January
Warned to be ready to evacuate the camp as the Russians were getting close. Packed case, packed as much food as we could, and scoffed the rest. I was ready to carry case, food parcel, and blanket wrapped round neck. Had to wear flying boots as no ordinary ones were available. [These were lambswool lined, loose fitting and not designed for walking.] Very close Russian bombing. Sleepless night as we had to be ready to move off any minute. [At this time I had been issued with an identity tag and was officially 'on the books'. In the event of death, the lower half was broken off and kept for records, the other half was buried with the body.]

19 January
Departed 0500 in bitter weather, after hanging about in the cold for a long time. Marched all day, 27km, to Winterfeld. Had to eat snow as no water was available. Spent the night wedged in a very small barn. Hardly slept at all.

20 January
Wakened 5 a.m. and set off again. Marched all morning, 12km, to an abandoned brick factory at Karlsruhe. Warm and dry. Had something to eat, a brew of coffee, then went to sleep. Feet very bad with blisters, so tied boots on with wire. Started dragging case inside the lid of another abandoned one, towing it along with a bootlace. Much kit jettisoned by the side of the road. Left 2000, as the Russians were getting close again. Marched without stopping all night.

21 January
Crossed the Oder 0500 – bridge mined, ready to blow up. Stopped in a village, but no accommodation was available, so pressed on another 5km, making 41km in all. Many chaps dropped out during the night because of bad feet and exhaustion. Arrived Barrkwitz (sic) 1100. Got bed space in a barn and had something to eat. A bull charged in scattering everybody. When it was ejected, went to sleep.

22 January
Roused 0300, as the Russians were still pressing on. The Germans had a bit of a job getting the chaps moving again, and there was some shooting. Pushed on 16 km to Jenkwitz, arriving at noon. Moved some cattle out of barn and got a bed space organised. Warm but very damp and smelling strongly of cattle. Ration of 1 cup of coffee, ½ a biscuit and marge. [Coffee issued by the Germans was made of acorns roasted and ground up, and with milk and sugar from Red Cross parcels was not too bad at all.]

23 January
Left 0900. Marched 25km to Wansen. Small bread issue and 1 cup of soup.

24 January
Spent the day at Wansen, trying to get some rest.

25 January
Left 0600 and marched 27km to Heidersdorf.

26 January
Stayed the day at Heidersdorf. Ration 2/5 of a loaf, and marge.

27 January
Left 1100 and marched 24 km to Pfaffendorf, arriving at 1700. Small barn, wretched cramped bed space, underneath a ladder – grain falling down from above all the time. Made up a double bed with John.

28 January
Left 0400; did 22 km to Stansdort (sic), in bitter weather, a fierce cold wind and driving snow. [You could rake your finger-nails down your face and not feel a thing, a real blizzard.] Arrived noon, dead-beat. Ration 4 biscuits and ½ cup of soup. [The German soup was watery in the extreme. There were two varieties – a) made from shredded dried turnip, and b) a less popular variety made from a very dark green cabbage of some sort, like spinach, known to the consumers as Whispering Grass, after a well-known song at the time.] Cold uncomfortable bed space. Left 1830, still dragging case – nothing jettisoned. Collected 2 packets of hard biscuits (8 in all) outside a town after 3 km. Walked all night through a fierce blizzard – heavy snow, roads sometimes blocked, so had to clamber through drifts. Much transport abandoned. Many more chaps dropped out during this night.

29 January
Very heavy going. Slow halting freezing march. Arrived Peterwitz 0200 in an exhausted condition. Got a good warm ample bed space; made a double bed with John and turned in, too tired even to wait for soup from the field kitchen.

30 and 31 January
Spent at Peterwitz, resting.

1 February
Left 1000 and did 17km to Prausnitz. Snow thawed half way, so had to start carrying case, and found it very heavy. Small dirty farmyard, absolutely crowded. However, got a good dry bed space upstairs in a

barn, by a water cistern. Much brewing of coffee and porridge on fires in the farmyard. Soup twice a day from field kitchens.

2, 3, 4 February

At Prausnitz. On the evening of the 4th issued with marching rations – 1/3 loaf, 1/3 tin of liver pate, and some margarine. Although you could not style our progress as 'marching'. We shambled along in a dejected shabby column, with German guards along the sides accompanied by Alsatians.

5 February

Roused 0400, left 0700 and did 7 km to Goldberg. Slight rain. Stole some sugar beet along the way and gnawed at it. Packed into cattle trucks at the station, 55 men to a truck, and locked in. [These trucks, common on the Continent, bore the legend 40 hommes, 8 chevaux, so we were well over the limit. There was not even enough room for everyone to sit down. There was a small barred window in each corner, also one large tin for toilet purposes. The vicinity of this tin was not rated very highly.] Travel slow, with many long halts of 7 to 8 hours.

6, 7, 8 February

On the train. Very hungry. Ate some spoonfuls of flour, barley and sugar mixed, from a cocoa tin. No water. Bought a crust of bread from Eddie, which he found behind the track, for tobacco.

9 February

Arrived at Luckenwalde, 23 miles SW of Berlin, 0800, feeling very weak. Marched 5 km up to the camp, Stalag IIIA. Much hanging about. Brewed coffee. Queued up all afternoon and had a hot shower. Got a billet with John – not too bad a position, on the floor on wood-straw, underneath a window. Warm and light anyhow, and room to stretch out. Porridge and potatoes, from the Germans, and a cup of soup from our own field kitchen.

10 February

Changed into pyjamas and washed dirty clothes. Had a shave.

11 February

German rations 1/6 loaf, 5 potatoes, 1/3 litre of soup, and German tea in the morning and evening. [This tea was a herbal mixture, and with milk and sugar made a reasonable drink. A count was held in the mornings early, to find who wanted their tea brewed and who wanted the mixture dry, to smoke – it was just like herbal tobacco. The potatoes were grown in a field near the camp, the crop being fertilised with the contents of the latrine (or 'abort' in German), and were boiled in their skins.]

12 February

Wrote home. [This letter, however, did not arrive.] Bad attack of dysentery, which made me even weaker. Nearly everybody had it. [This was brought on by eating raw or undercooked food, insufficient bulk, the freezing conditions of the march, and by general weakness and lack of resistance. For the first few days at Luckenwalde, everyone just lay on the floor, listless and apathetic, except for occasional dashes to the abort – not everyone made it in time.]

14 February

Usual day, weak with hunger and dysentery.

16 February and thereafter

A succession of wretched days, very little food. Listened to BBC news brought round and read out daily in each barrack block, received on illicit radio. This was known to the Germans, but they failed to unearth the set. Anyway, even if they did, there were others in reserve. Shaved and washed once a week. Two roll-call parades in the freezing cold every day, between 30 minutes and an hour each.

27 February

On fatigue. Slept last night fully dressed it was so cold. Called 6 a.m., collected keevil, [a tub used from bringing up the barrack block's daily ration of soup] and went down for tea. Parade, breakfast, another parade for blanket inspections. Had a wash and shave. Then Jeff Orr and Leach's gunner came in and sat and talked till soup time. They say

F/O Bacon, flying as second pilot, had his time too that night on Duisburg. I wonder what Hopeful King and his lot will do about getting another skipper. Afternoon parade 5pm. After that Red X parcel issue: morale went up 100%. The issue was 1 American parcel between 4 men. When we got in from parade we shared it out: it was just like Christmas time for us. … After share out had a good tea and felt really grand. Then sirens went and lights went out, so I made my bed and turned in.

Parcel issue was not usually as convenient as this – it was often one between seven or one between nine, which made sharing difficult. Some people made nearly all the contents of their parcels into a sort of solid cake, known as 'glop', but we preferred to use one item at a time.

Chapter Fifteen

Red Tape, Muddling and Disappointment

In 1982 I went to a Stalag Luft VII reunion at Nottingham, and this is the menu and an excerpt of the address to those present. Note the amounts stated in the menu, maintaining the tradition of difficult share-outs. How do you share six prunes between ten?

Menu

Soup of the day (Pea Flour. American No. 10)

Meat and Vegetable (English Red Cross)
(One tin between twelve guests)
One 1/8' slice Spam (Treet or Prem)
Mixed Vegetable (1/4 tin per person)
One dessertspoon peas with crisp black beetles
One boiled potato – in jacket – unwashed
IF YOU REQUIRE GRAVY WILL YOU PLEASE SAVE SOME OF YOUR SOUP.

Dried Apricots or Prunes (Six between ten guests)
OR
Tinned marmalade pudding (One tin between nine)
Klim bash

1/12 small loaf black bread or two water biscuits
1/8 oz. Oleomargarine

Limburg fish cheese (Left-overs from 1981 reunion)

Acorn coffee with molasses and condensed milk

THERE WILL BE A GASH ISSUE OF CHEESE AT 22.45 Hrs.

Cigarette issue tomorrow at 06.00 Hrs

The East Midlands Branch of The Royal Air Forces Ex-Prisoner of War Association welcomes you to the second Stalag Luft VII reunion at the White Eagle Club, Nottingham. Saturday 20th March 1982.

Guests of Honour: Rev. John Collins, C. of E. Padre Stalag Luft VII. Bob Trett, Hon. Secretary E. Mid. Branch, RAF ex POWA and, of course, their good ladies.

Once again we are pleased to welcome you to this gathering of ex-guests of the Reich Holiday Camp Stalag Luft VII, which was, as we all know, situated in the lovely Silesian forests. Apart from the famous International football matches, facilities were available for indulging in various other sporting activities, such as: Louse Hunting, Dog walking to Kreuzburg [sic], Goon Baiting and Ferreting. For those interested in shooting one had only to step over that low wire to be able to participate. Hiking and other Winter Sports were catered for during January and February in 1945.
The staff in the camp were very attentive to all of us. They even stood for hours in tall towers watching for forest fires so that we would not be in any danger. If during a ball game you were unfortunate enough to lose your ball over the low wire the blue-coat in the tower would make sure that no traffic was coming before motioning you to cross the wire. Can you ever forget that luxury train journey to Luckenwalde? What comfort – only 66 to a wagon. …

We are particularly pleased to see that 'Man amongst men' John Collins, and his wife Helen, with us again. May they come for many years more. How many of us owe our very lives to him? His encouragement and example kept many of us marching on across

> Silesia when all we wanted to do was sit down and freeze. How many times did we hear him say, 'Only another 3 or 4 kilometres to our next stopping place', 'The next village is only down the road. We are stopping there'. Well done John. Thank you. ...

Klim was dried powdered milk from American Red Cross parcels. The Limburg fish cheese is worthy of note. It came in wooden boxes that, when opened, revealed about twenty oval flattish cakes covered with some sort of skin, and gave off an appalling stench. The only way of eating this delicacy was to strip off the skin, liberally douse the content with pepper and salt, hold your nose and consume the cheese with the utmost dispatch. There were not many takers, so there was plenty for those with stomachs strong enough to take it, but over-consumption could precipitate an attack of the squitters.

A few other items from this programme need further description. Among the 'sporting activities' we find louse hunting. Lice thrived in the crowded insanitary conditions. If you have not had the privilege of encountering any, they were flat dirty-grey insects, hard-shelled – if you squeezed one between your fingers it had no effect. They lurked in the seams of clothing, so had to be winkled out and crushed between thumb-nails, and there was a little spot of blood if they had recently fed. They carried, of course, the germs of typhus, and the Germans were always much perturbed to hear of increased infestation – any plague would have swept like wildfire through the camp and while I don't suppose the effect on prisoners would have worried them a great deal, it would eventually have affected the Germans themselves.

Dog-walking to Kreuzberg. Kreuzburg was the nearest town and any prisoners requiring dental or medical treatment had to walk there, accompanied by a guard and the inevitable Alsatian.

Goon-baiting, which practice accounted for the majority of the inmates of the 'cooler', was a popular sport aimed at making the Germans feel uncomfortable. I don't think it took place much in Army camps, as soldiers were used to taking orders and doing as they were told, but air-crew were more rebellious, independent spirits inclined to follow their own dictates. In a bomber crew, for instance, the pilot was the captain, and any decision must ultimately be his, but he rarely had to give orders;

in case of necessity, he took advice from the appropriate crew member, a specialist who knew more than he did, weighed up the advice and then made his decision, but it was more a matter of consensus than orders. Goon-baiting usually consisted of telling the Germans that their country was finished, in ruins, that they had been misled, and that things were going to be tough for them.

Ferreting came into the same category of making the Germans feel uncomfortable and inferior. A ferret was a member of the camp staff who prowled around looking for illegal activity, and was dealt with by the 'duty pilot's system'. The airman on duty accompanied by a runner and a tail, would take up position at the entrance to the compound. When a ferret appeared, his name and time of arrival would be written down, making sure that he knew what was happening. The runner set off to visit each hut and call out, 'Goon in the block.' The 'tail' followed closely behind the ferret, making his presence felt. If the ferret turned round and remonstrated with him he melted away into the crowd and a replacement took over. The object of all this was to inform the Germans that the compound was our preserve and that they only came in under sufferance.

And now a tribute to Captain John Collins, the Stalag Luft VII padre. Read again the paragraph that describes him; every word is true, but words alone cannot do him justice. Where most of us were trudging along, heads down, concerned only for ourselves, he would appear at different parts of the column, sometimes speeding up, sometimes slowing down, so that everybody had a share of inspiration from his company. I can picture him now, face reddened by the blizzard, always cheerful, always optimistic, his arm round the shoulder of a man beginning to despair, carrying his gear for a little way as well as his own, then a pat on the back and off to find someone else. And the man he had just left thought, 'If he can bloody well do it, so can I.' Truly a 'man among men', and I am sure his inspiration did save lives.

The following pages are a continuing day to day account of Henry's experiences, which is a combination of his edited 'diary' entries and other thoughts (in brackets).

8 March

Issued today with 1 American No. 10 Red X parcel each – even more like Xmas. Tins unpunctured. John and I are keeping one intact in case we have to march again, or for when the parcel supply runs out (although we have been promised 1/week for next 5 weeks). We are living pretty well now, and time is passing amazingly quickly – we go to church every Sunday evening and it seems no time at all between services. Almost all day is taken up cooking and there is hardly any time for anything else. When parcels came Germans took our range away, out of spite I suppose, to stop us getting full value from them. Se we set to and made 'Smokey Joes': these made up of 2 Klim tins, one on top of other to create a draught, and a salmon tin (perforated) set into top to act as a grate. Fuel is cardboard and chips of wood, fed in one at a time and allowed to burn up to get full value. I act as permanent stoker and blower and John watches grub! Here is our daily programme in cooking line: Breakfast of ½ daily bread portion, with jam, cheese and peanut butter. After about an hour comes ritual of 'brewing up', or 'having a hot brew' – tea, cocoa, or coffee. When that is done another meal of some sort – fried bread and Spam, or stewed prunes and cream. Nothing further till German soup issue (1 cup) about 2 pm. Potatoes come up shortly afterwards. These John and I put together, peel, and mash in a saucepan, adding a spoon of Klim, some salt and good helping of Jerry marg, and some spice: then we add a portion of a tin of Spam, bully, or Meat and Beans, and mix lot together. This is cooked up on Smokey Joe and consumed straight away. Much washing of utensils. Tea after parade – ½ ration of bread, with cheese, jam and peanut butter again. Turn in about 7.30 before lights go out because of nightly air raid on Berlin, 40 miles away. 1 oz of chocolate each in bed. That's not bad, is it? A hell of a lot better than Jerry rations.

13 March

Another issue of American Red X No. 10 parcel each. We swopped our cocoa for 2 choc, peanut butter for Rosemilk Pâté, biscuits for cereal, and prunes for raisins. Bought 1 packet prunes at Exchange, for biscuits. The weather has turned out glorious last few days, and that together with good food makes me feel pretty good. Just after we arrived here I was so weak that everytime I stood up things went black before my eyes and I could only walk a few steps dragging my feet along ground – everybody was same. We were all so antipathetic that all we did was sit around all day doing nothing and feeling wretched.

16 March
Germans cut rations to potatoes every other day, 1/6 of a loaf a day, and half margarine and sugar rations.

21 March
Cold. High wind blowing dust all over the place. Difficult day for Smokey Joe – cut up a Klim tin and made a windshield for him. Issue of 1 American Red Cross No. 10 per man – prunes, chocolate, peanut butter, tuna, plum jam, Camel cigarettes. Swapped chocolate for raisins. News good today – Worms, Ludwigshafen, Neustadt and Homburg taken. Germans in chaos all along the line.

24 March
Twenty-two today. They'll probably be thinking of me at home and wondering what sort of a birthday I'm having. [There had been no news from them from 19 December to 6 March, so they had only heard less than three weeks before.] Shifted dirty straw from bedspace and burned it, in response to an anti-typhus purge by the Germans, so we lay on the bare boards thereafter.

27 March
Issue of the dreaded Limburg fish cheese. Got a bundle of wood from a Russian for 2 cigarettes. Diphtheria broke out in our barrack block – enforced gurgling and opening of windows.

30 March
Good Friday. Washed, shaved, and put on hair grease. [This was an issue of an evil looking black grease, much resembling axle grease, which it may well have been. Goodness knows why they issued it.] Cleaned shoes. Parade by main gate 0920 for church – The Seven Words from the Cross, by Captain Collins.

2 April
Day dragged interminably. Made some prune jam, but it was cold and windy, a bad day for Smokey Joes.

5 April
Issue of 1 American Red Cross No. 10 per man. One more and they will all be finished – time to tighten belts again. Destruction of German rail system and rolling stock by the RAF prevents supply of more parcels.

11 April
This evening, it was announced that a partial evacuation from Luckenwalde would begin tomorrow. All officers going and NCOs from Barrack 3 and 33 from Barrack 7. John and I volunteered to be among the 33 because we thought the others might not get transport and would have to march. Packed kit and shared out food for carrying; we had a whole cage full of tins of food stored up, a little from every parcel.

12 April
Called out to move off after soup 1100. Much checking and roll-calls. Search, just before which we had to get cracking in a hurry and puncture all our tins. Nothing taken, except they took one of John's blankets. Marched down to Luckenwalde station. We had our blower with us. John insisted on bringing it and just outside the station we set it down and had a hot brew, which was very welcome although it was a hot day. Issue of 40 cigarettes per man. Entrained in cattle trucks, 40 per truck. Stole porage oats from a nearby train. [Looking up through the floorboards of a truck we saw sacks inside. On being slit open with a knife a steady stream of oats came through a wide crack, which was much appreciated by those in the vicinity.] Sleeping-space cramped, but I have been in worse. Very hot and stuffy – no ventilation.

13 April
Up 0600 and brewed up. Had bread, then stewed prunes. Talk by Wing Command[er] in charge of the party. Bombing of the line down at Treuenbrietzen means we can't leave here for some time. BBC news read out during evening. Also it was announced we go back to camp tomorrow.

14 April
Up 0600. Porridge, then bread. Results of trading with German civvies – ½ loaf, 2 onions, 6 eggs, 30 saccharine tablets, and 4lbs of potatoes for 65 cigarettes and 2 bars of soap. Marched back to camp and got organised in our same barrack. While we were away, 2 RAF chaps shot trying to climb the wire – 'stir-crazy', I suppose.

15 April
Issue of 1 parcel between 2. That is the last now. Water turned off nearly all day.

18 April
News good today. Our advance appears to have slowed down, but the Russians have started a big push on the Berlin front, and are doing well. Organisation going ahead for running the camp ourselves when the Germans leave.

20 April
Bombing of Potsdam and Wriezenburg (sic) by US heavies. Lovely fine day. Clouds of smoke over target. Made out a list of food in stock and rationed it to last 5 weeks. This evening there was a feeling in the air that something was going to happen, but there was no definite news. Russian artillery plainly heard, red glows in the sky.

21 April
Heard German staff moving out with lorries, tractors and cars during the night. Not called out on parade this morning. A few German guards still left, but not many. Russian tank crews brought in – short imprisonment for them. Looting of German staff quarters, but not much to be had. Prisoners' record cards from the camp offices were distributed. Dull rainy day. Wing Commander Beamont [who later became chief pilot for English Electric, and was in charge of test-flying Canberras and Lightnings], announced that the Germans had left, the camp was surrounded, and the Russians were fighting in Luckenwalde and Juterborg [sic] last night.

22 April
Slept fully dressed last night in case we had to make a dash for the trucks. French and British flags flying at the gate, and a big red Russian one near the cookhouse. White flags at intervals round the perimeter barbed wire. At 1030 Russian tanks and lorries arrived in force. All the Russian prisoners were given rifles and moved out straight away, anxious to kill Germans. [Russia was not a signatory to the Geneva Convention for treatment of prisoners of war, and they had a terrible time of it in the camp, almost starved and worked to death. The same treatment was accorded to German prisoners held by the Russians.] Artillery duel just outside the camp in the evening, between Germans hiding in a wood and a party of Russians.

Over the course of the next few days Henry's main preoccupation was the gathering, cooking and consuming of food.

23 April
Frankie on guard 5–6, made us a brew when he came in. Had a wash at pump – cold, miserable, rainy day. Back to bed till 0830. Up and brewed up cereal, prunes, raisins, milk, sugar and marg, which made a good thick meal. Frankie brought in another brew. Did an hr's patrol at fence, then in and cooked spam and chips, after which Frankie brought in yet another brew.

24 April
Another day of good eating. The Russians have placed us on first priority after their own front-line troops for food: plenty of meat (rabbit) in soup. 1/8 tin German meat. Good potato ration. New bread. Some of 1 Canadian Red X parcel/4 men. Whacked it out, meanwhile consuming biscuits and chocolate.

On 25 April Henry recorded: 'Still no news of moving. Another day of good eating.' He also received an issue of forty-five cigarettes, swopping forty 'with a yank for 2 ozs of tobacco'. His friend John was able to add to their menu, managing to retrieve some rhubarb from the Kommandantur garden, which they enjoyed for tea.

27 April

Up early, washed, and brewed up: back to bed. Up at 0900, out through wire with John, Stinger, Bill and Frankie, and made our way across country down to Luckenwalde. Pushed our way into 2 bakeries where I got 1 ½ loaves and John got 1. Walked around town for about an hr. Got into French civil camp and spoke to froggies and got some coffee to drink and tin American cheese for 20 cigs. Back through woods to camp. Had ¼ loaf each, soup, brewed up, had rhubarb and custard, more bread, and another brew. News through of link up Americans and Russians, but none of leaving here yet. It looks as if it will be some time yet.

29 April

Rainy. After soup, got nabbed for a job over in stores – shifting out sacks of dirty Russian rags and pretty wet working out in rain. After job was over got a bowl of soup and 1/3 loaf, then had a hot shower. Spent rest of afternoon cooking – rhubarb jam, potatoes and salmon, and bread pudding. At 6 had to go on 4 hour duty as runner up at HQ – not much doing. Came off at 10, had a brew and some bread, then turned in.

30 April

Went for a walk through the woods with John and Frankie in evening and did about 5 miles. Discovered 2 crash-landed FW190s.

1 May

Many Germans in this area and heavy fighting going on. Germans who escaped from Berlin still fighting on here. 120,000 prisoners taken today in this vicinity. In the evening went for a short walk with John again and came across 2 dead German soldiers shot by the Russians the night before by machine guns. Covered with blood and horrible chest wounds. The move to the Adolf Hitler Lager has been cancelled because refugees have looted and destroyed the place.

3 May

Dull cold day. This evening American war correspondent in camp from W. Front. He said we have not moved because they did not know the way was clear of fighting. He is taking a roll back with him, and a representative will be sent tomorrow to Gen. Eisenhower to see about getting us away from here. Bread rations down to 1/7 loaf and getting hungry again. Red X food almost finished.

4 May

Shaved, had breakfast, then a brew, then soup. Set off about noon with John, Eddie, and Frank on a private foraging party. Headed through Frankenforde to Felgentreu, where there was nothing doing, we got warned off by a Jerry with a red armband. Headed to Zülichendorf, picking up seed potatoes, across a field on the way. The Jerry loosed off a rifle at us so we packed that up and made off towards a village. Split up when we got there. I got some potatoes, a lot of rhubarb, 2 jars preserved fruit and 1 jar meat from larder in a German house. Frankie got a jar of fruit and a jar of meat. John and Eddie got between them 3 chickens, 9 eggs, and lot of potatoes, and a few onions. Heavy to carry back and had a brew on arrival. News of American lorries, 70 of them coming tomorrow to take us away. Much scoffing going on. Sold Stinger a chicken for a D bar. Had bread and thick jam, then cherries, cream and sugar. Got a bucket and started boiling the chicken and did it for 1 ½ hours. Then the lights went out, so turned in and got into bed. So excited over moving that I couldn't get to sleep for a long time.

On one of our private foraging parties, John and I fell in with some Polish prisoners who had been employed at the factory making V-1 flying bombs. None of us could speak the other side's language, so everything was done by signs. We went back to their billet with them, and they produced enamel mugs and bottles of spirit, looking like lemon barley water, which we gathered was fuel for the flying bombs, and must have been almost pure alcohol. Some was poured on a table, a match applied and it went 'whoomph'. We imbibed a fair quantity of this, and were soon blotto. We staggered back to camp and sagged down to sleep it off: woke up with a raging thirst and had a drink of water. This had the effect of reactivating the spirit, setting the whole business in motion again, so we were back to square one.

Staff Sergeant Nettell, 'Stinger', of the Glider Pilot Regiment, was the senior NCO in our hut, and something of a comedian. Rumours were rife towards the end, and prisoners were somewhat apprehensive about what the Germans might have in store for them. One day Stinger came into the hut, called for silence, and announced, 'Everyone in this hut is to parade outside in five minutes' time – to march down to the stores, to draw picks and shovels, to dig their own graves.' I thought, 'So it's come to that, has it?' There was a stunned silence for a moment, then laughter broke out. Stinger and his jokes again!

5 May
Red Cross lorries arrived and evacuated the sick.

6 May
The Russians were very reluctant to let us go, and our impatience mounted. A convoy of American lorries arrived in the afternoon to take us away, but the Russians sent them away empty and put armed guards on the fence, so we were still prisoners but with different custodians. About 11pm a report came from the Senior British Officer. I was almost asleep, and the only words that made any impression on me were, 'red tape, muddling and disappointment'.

7 May
Decided to get out while the going was as good as it was going to get. Departed at noon in company with John, Frankie, Stinger, Bill and a few others. After walking 10km to Zülichendorf we met another convoy of lorries heading for the camp, one of which picked us up, turned round, and headed towards the west, finishing up at a POW reception centre at Schönebeck, on the Elbe, in what was a Junkers aircraft factory. So we were once again in safe hands. The war ended the next day with unconditional German surrender.

11 May
Embarked in lorries and proceeded via Magdeburg and Brunswick to an ex-German fighter aerodrome at Hildesheim. Had a hot shower and a de-lousing. In this latter operation, an orderly put the nozzle of a large syringe down the front of one's trousers and sent a blast of DDT round the interior. Assigned to an aircraft party. Got a Red Cross parcel

containing soap (toilet, tooth and shaving), shaving brush, razor and blades, two handkerchiefs, toothbrush, face-cloth, toilet bag, 50 cigarettes and ½ lb of chocolate. Soup, bread, coffee and a K-ration for tea.

12 May
Called out to the aerodrome after breakfast. A steady stream of Dakotas was coming in, filling up and taking off again. Took off 1600, flew over the devastated areas of the Ruhr, and landed at Brussels 1800. Tea and biscuits from the Naafi waggon. Transported in lorries to 42 RHU at Louvain, about 12 miles out. Deloused once again.

13 May
Taken back to Brussels airport in the afternoon, got aboard a Dakota and flew back to England via Ostend and the Thames Estuary. Landed at Wing, near Aylesbury. Deloused yet again – they must have thought these lice were pretty hardy characters, to have survived two previous assaults. After more tea and biscuits transported to Bicester aerodrome, where we stayed the night. Bacon and eggs, bread and marmalade, and tea.

14 May
Train to Cosford, near Wolverhampton. Given new uniform and kit, went through documentation, given ration cards and leave passes, and pay. Medical exam.

15 May
Left late in the afternoon, travelled through the night, and arrived in Reading 0430. Two hours to wait for train to Twyford, and another half hour one to Henley. When I arrived home the rest of the family were still in bed and I had to knock them up.

There followed several days of seeing old friends and places again, writing to parents of the rest of my crew, playing golf, servicing my motorcycle and generally relaxing and feeling glad to be home again and to be able to wander as I pleased.

Shortly after the war Henry applied to become a member of the Caterpillar Club and was successful. On 11 July his leave expired and he returned to Cosford for a matter of a few days before enjoying some further extended leave. On 29 August he arrived at RAF Wittering but had 'nothing much to do'. During this period he also took time to visit the father of his bomb aimer and family of his mid-upper gunner. Henry applied for his release from the RAF in January 1946, which was granted, and he returned to Reading University where he graduated with a BA Honours degree in French in the summer of 1947. Henry then embarked upon a teaching career, at a small public school in Leatherhead, then a grammar school near Reading, followed by five years teaching in Kenya and then the Queen's Girls' School in Wisbech. In 1949 Henry married Joan, who sadly passed away in 1976.

In 2010 Henry visited the crash site of his Halifax, and was able to view some of the wreckage of his aircraft, bringing home a section of panel. Henry also went to pay his respects at the graves of his crew at Venray War Cemetery. He was the only survivor on that fateful night in December 1944. 'It is a peaceful spot, surrounded by trees, and beautifully maintained by the Imperial War Graves Commission (sic). The tombstones are kept clean and in front of each one is a flowering plant.' Henry remains extremely active, bungee jumping and hang-gliding being recent adventures. Yes – bungee jumping. Go on to youtube.com and enter '90-year-old bungee jump Wisbech'. Remarkable!

Acknowledgements

Particular thanks extend, of course, to the former Kriegies David, Albert, Charles, Reg and Henry for willingly sharing their stories, and also to Bob Ankerson for agreeing to write the foreword. A special thank you also to my mother, Jennifer Darlow, for her work on the transcribing of interviews.

I also extend my appreciation to the following people for their assistance in putting this book together: Dr Robert Owen, Sylvia Forder, Clare Gelnar, Steve Drawbridge, Deborah Evans, Gillian Paterson, and Debra Boraston.

Endnotes

1. The aircraft remained in the loch until 1985 when it was finally salvaged, and restored, to eventually end up as part of the aircraft museum at Brooklands, the former motor racing circuit. It was during a family visit to Brooklands in 2014, where I gave a two-hour recorded interview for their archives, that we were looking over a Wellington fuselage and discovered that it was the same aircraft that had featured in the Loch Ness incident. I was invited by one of the curators to occupy the rear turret, but owing to advancing years, coupled with the fact that the central walkway had been removed (thus increasing the effective height of the mainspar by about eighteen inches), I was unable to surmount the obstacle. However, my great-grandson Benjamin was eagerly watching my efforts, so I motioned to him to take my place and within a few seconds his smiling face was beaming at me through the Perspex of the turret. Little did I realise, that the rear turret of that aircraft from Lossiemouth would, in 2014, be occupied by my great-grandson.

2. Some years after the war, Bill was working in his office when he received a message from the gatekeeper that there was a friend waiting to see him. When Bill arrived at the gate he was amazed to see the tall figure of Louis, in priest's garb. Louis had, in fact, taken the cloth some years previously and, as he was visiting England, decided to track Bill down. He spent the night with Bill and his wife and they talked into the small hours, reminiscing on the war years and their brief time together on the squadron. As a result of his war injuries, Bill was repatriated in 1943 and, on returning home, he was passed fit for non-operational flying duties. He attended the RAF Central Navigation School where he obtained very high marks on his course and he was commissioned, and flew, as a navigation instructor until the end of the European war. My wife Barbara and I went to stay with Bill at his mother's house, in Weymouth soon after the European war had ended and we spent one night scooting around the town in Bill's small MG car. It was only a two-seater so I had to sit on the folded-back canvas hood when we pub-crawled around town. In those days service personnel proliferated and everyone was bent on having a great rip-roaring time. In London, one could not walk many yards without meeting someone you knew and the alcohol flowed and was drunk with reckless abandon.

3. Quoted in *Footprints in the Sands of Time. RAF Bomber Command Prisoners-of-War in Germany 1939–1945* by Oliver Clutton-Brock (Grub Street, 2003) and from *The Trial of German Major War Criminals* (HMSO, London, 1946–51).

4. Information on Jim Cooper kindly supplied by No. 617 Squadron historian Dr Robert Owen.

5. *Footprints in the Sands of Time. RAF Bomber Command Prisoners-of-War in Germany 1939–1945* by Oliver Clutton-Brock (Grub Street, 2003) with the Zemke quote coming from *Zemke's Stalag* by Hubert Zemke (Airlife Publishing, 1991).

Index

Units

A

B

C

D

E

F

G

H

I

J

K

L

U

V

W

Y

Z